Fergus Linehan
Director, Edinburgh International Festival

The Edinburgh International Festival is immensely proud of the Edinburgh Festival Chorus, the only performing component of the Festival itself. Over the course of 50 years it has thrilled us and garnered the praise of audiences, conductors and orchestras from all over the world for the power, scale and energy of its performances.

The Chorus stands as a superb example of the artistic heights that can be reached when people join in a creative community. Each member enjoys singing as an amateur and yet together they are world-class and stand shoulder to shoulder with the best professional choruses in the world.

The Festival and the city of Edinburgh are connected, too, through this Chorus. The Festival is brought into the lives and homes of the Chorus members and their families through their participation, and these 130 singers, largely from Edinburgh, take centre stage at a number of concerts each summer putting local performers at the heart of the Festival's music programme.

The Edinburgh Festival Chorus is a rich and wonderful presence in the Festival, which we look forward to celebrating for many years to come.

Christopher Bell
Chorus Master, Edinburgh Festival Chorus

The Edinburgh Festival Chorus' 50th anniversary allows the Festival, its audiences and EFC members an opportunity to look back on, and be proud of, a great and distinguished history. I count myself privileged to have been Chorus Master since the 2008 Festival, working with the talented EFC singers and some of the world's finest orchestras, conductors and soloists on great repertoire – part of the EFC's history, and helping to shape its future. The energy of Tuesday evening rehearsals; the buzz when we meet orchestras and conductors; the thrill of performances in the Usher Hall; the roar of the audience's approval – all these add up to a most satisfying life in singing.

We must also take the opportunity to look to the future and see how the EFC can develop and grow, while maintaining and enhancing its reputation. Life in 2015 is very different to how it was in 1965, and increased work commitments mean there are different challenges in recruiting and fielding singers for a month-long festival in the summer. But as its four Chorus Masters and a multitude of singers have found over 50 years, the rewards for this time and effort are immense, so we must continue to mount exceptional performances, and go on to even greater things, becoming an even stronger cultural force both nationally and internationally.

Contents

Editor David Kettle
Project Manager Kathy Crawford Hay
Designers Dawid Nabiałek, Marcin Potępski
Edinburgh International Festival Head of Communications Susie Gray
Edinburgh Festival Chorus Manager Helen MacLeod

For the Edinburgh International Festival
Festival Director and Chief Executive Fergus Linehan
Managing Director Joanna Baker
Planning Director Roy Luxford
Marketing and Communications Director Jackie Westbrook
Artists Co-ordinator Drew Young

For the Edinburgh Festival Chorus
Chorus Master Christopher Bell
Trustees David Arulanantham, Kathy Crawford Hay, Elizabeth Currie, David Hewitson, Ivor Klayman

Thanks to John Anderton, David Arulanantham, Anne Backhouse, Kenneth Ballantine, Frank Barclay, Martina von Bargen, Ronnie Barnes, David Bonnar, Jenny Brockie, Barbara Brodie, Valerie Bryan, Derek Calder, Peter Cannell, Roger Chalmers-Lang, Malcolm and Susan Crosby, Nancy Crook, Elizabeth Currie, Liliana Currie, Rosamund Davidson, Margaret Donaldson, William Durran, Jim Eunson, Dorothy Fairweather, Ann Firth, Tori Graham, Anne Grindley,
David Jones, Jack Kirk, Ivor Klayman, family of Anne Laurie, Martha and Susan Lester-Cribb, Janet McKenzie, Catriona McDonald, Andrew Moore, Royal Scottish National Orchestra, Lorraine Veitch Rutherford, Andrew Scott, Mike Smith, Jennifer Swan, Lesley Walker, James Walls, Brenda and Raymond Williamson

Inside covers: Edinburgh Festival Chorus 2015 singers, photographed by Stuart Armitt

Additional photography by Kathy Crawford Hay

Published by the Edinburgh International Festival, The Hub, Castlehill, Edinburgh EH1 2NE

ISBN 978–0–9932082–0–1

© 2015 Edinburgh International Festival. Reproduction in whole or in part is forbidden without the written permission of the publishers.

Printed by Allander, Edinburgh

Edinburgh International Festival is supported by

·EDINBVRGH·
THE CITY OF EDINBURGH COUNCIL

CREATIVE SCOTLAND
ALBA | CHRUTHACHAIL

Charity No SC004694

Courtesy Royal Scottish National Orchestra archive

The Edinburgh Festival Chorus in 1965 (above) and in 2015 (bottom right)

Courtesy EIF archive

In the beginning

It was vision, determination, raw talent and a striving for excellence – as well as a collection of extraordinary individuals – that established what became the Edinburgh Festival Chorus in 1965. David Kettle looks back to where it all began

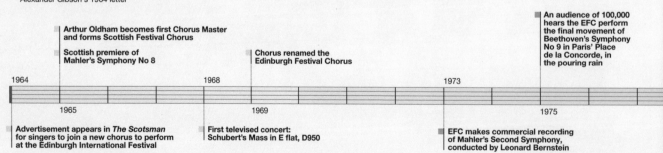

Momentous message:
Alexander Gibson's 1964 letter

It all started with a letter – and with sky-high ambitions. In August 1964, Alexander Gibson, then Principal Conductor of the Scottish National Orchestra, wrote to Lord Harewood, Director of the Edinburgh International Festival, with plans for a new chorus that would perform at the opening concert of the following year's Festival. Right from the start, this new choir should be open to all, but it should also expect the very best. 'It is not good enough to extract at random sections from the Glasgow and Edinburgh Choral Unions, Scottish Opera Chorus etc and call it a Scottish Festival Chorus. An invitation must be extended to everybody interested in joining and they must be auditioned by a suitable panel of experts. We should set our sights high.'

Not only would the two men go on to establish what has become cherished as the Edinburgh International Festival's single continuous performing ensemble, but they'd do it with one of the grandest pieces of music ever conceived. 'It is vitally important,'

An audience of 100,000 hears the EFC perform the final movement of Beethoven's Symphony No 9 in Paris' Place de la Concorde, in the pouring rain

Arthur Oldham becomes first Chorus Master and forms Scottish Festival Chorus

Scottish premiere of Mahler's Symphony No 8

Chorus renamed the Edinburgh Festival Chorus

1964

1968

1973

1965

1969

1975

Advertisement appears in *The Scotsman* for singers to join a new chorus to perform at the Edinburgh International Festival

First televised concert: Schubert's Mass in E flat, D950

EFC makes commercial recording of Mahler's Second Symphony, conducted by Leonard Bernstein

1965 EIF Director Lord Harewood (third from left)
with (l-r) Galina Vishnevskaya, Dmitri Shostakovich and Mstislav Rostropovich

EFC co-founder,
conductor Alexander Gibson

Daniel Barenboim rehearses with the EFC, 1974

continued Gibson, 'that we choose a work of tremendous impact which demands large choral forces. If we are going to form a special Festival chorus we may just as well go the whole hog and put on the Mahler Eighth. There is no doubt in my mind that it would be a most exciting choice for the opening of the Festival. In other words, I am well and truly "steamed up" about it!'

Gibson's excitement is understandable. Mahler's monumental Eighth Symphony, dubbed the 'Symphony of a Thousand' because of the enormous orchestral and choral forces required to perform it, charts a remarkable spiritual journey to ultimate redemption ➔

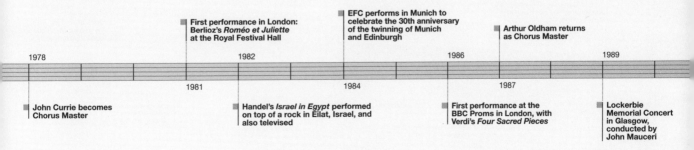

First performance in London:
Berlioz's *Roméo et Juliette*
at the Royal Festival Hall

EFC performs in Munich to
celebrate the 30th anniversary
of the twinning of Munich
and Edinburgh

Arthur Oldham returns
as Chorus Master

1978

1982

1986

1989

1981

1984

1987

John Currie becomes
Chorus Master

Handel's *Israel in Egypt* performed
on top of a rock in Eilat, Israel, and
also televised

First performance at the
BBC Proms in London, with
Verdi's *Four Sacred Pieces*

Lockerbie
Memorial Concert
in Glasgow,
conducted by
John Mauceri

through brotherhood and love. And it required an equally remarkable Chorus Master to put together a choir of more than 200 and to rehearse them for this gargantuan work.

Gibson and Harewood found just the man in Arthur Oldham, composer, conductor, former pupil of Britten, forthright in his opinions and a stickler for exceptional standards. 'It was Alex Gibson who telephoned me late one evening in 1965 to ask me to

meet him in Glasgow the following morning, since he had an important project to discuss,' Oldham wrote in his autobiography *Living with Voices*, published in 2000. 'The Festival director, Lord Harewood, had decided to create an indigenous Scottish Chorus and, accepting the advice of Gibson and others, was proposing to put me in charge of the project.'

Oldham was joined in the enterprise by the Music Director of Edinburgh's

Fettes College. 'I was singularly blessed in finding Michael Lester-Cribb, a superb accompanist. He remained with me, loyal, discreet, and always ready with sound advice when it was needed, for the whole of my some 30 years' association with the Festival Chorus,' wrote Oldham. And together, they set about auditioning hundreds of singers across the length and breadth of Scotland.

Tenor John Anderton, who sang with the Scottish Festival Chorus in its first concert and is still a member in 2015, remembers initial murmurings about the new choir. 'In September 1964 an advertisement appeared in *The Scotsman*: "Wanted: experienced singers to join the newly created Scottish Festival Chorus which will sing works at the Edinburgh Festival with world-renowned conductors, soloists and orchestras. If you are interested, please get in touch with the Chorus Master, Arthur Oldham."'

Oldham was surprised at the ease with which the Chorus' inaugural performance came together. 'It should have been a daunting task, but it was not,' he wrote. 'The music was so glorious, so incredibly well-written for the voices and so original, that the enthusiasm of my vast army of singers carried all before it and virtually assured the success of the opening concert of the 1965 Edinburgh Festival.'

Roger Perry, courtesy EIF archive

EIF Director Peter Diamand: making the EFC a permanent ensemble

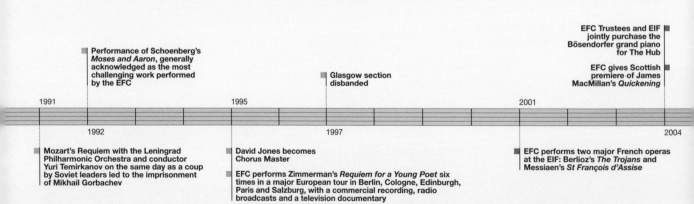

EFC Trustees and EIF jointly purchase the Bösendorfer grand piano for The Hub

EFC gives Scottish premiere of James MacMillan's *Quickening*

Performance of Schoenberg's *Moses and Aaron*, generally acknowledged as the most challenging work performed by the EFC

Glasgow section disbanded

1991

1995

2001

1992

1997

2004

Mozart's Requiem with the Leningrad Philharmonic Orchestra and conductor Yuri Temirkanov on the same day as a coup by Soviet leaders led to the imprisonment of Mikhail Gorbachev

David Jones becomes Chorus Master

EFC performs Zimmerman's *Requiem for a Young Poet* six times in a major European tour in Berlin, Cologne, Edinburgh, Paris and Salzburg, with a commercial recording, radio broadcasts and a television documentary

EFC performs two major French operas at the EIF: Berlioz's *The Trojans* and Messiaen's *St François d'Assise*

And a success that opening concert certainly was. Following months of auditions, rehearsals, the establishment of Chorus branches in Edinburgh, Glasgow and Aberdeen, travel between the three cities and occasional weekend get-togethers, the performance was a triumph. 'Gathered on stage on that memorable Sunday evening were the Scottish National Orchestra, eight international soloists, the Scottish Festival Chorus and a large boys' choir, all conducted by Alexander Gibson,' remembers Anderton. 'The stage was a mass of colour, with flowers in front of the orchestra, an array of supplementary brass on two stages erected either side of the organ decked with foliage, and the ladies of the Chorus who each wore individually coloured gowns instead of the customary black.'

It was such a resounding success that Harewood and incoming Festival Director Peter Diamand made the Scottish Festival Chorus a permanent ensemble, extending its remit to three performances the following year, and inviting international conductors to work with it.

One of the first of whom was the revered Herbert von Karajan, in 1967, who brought his equally revered Berlin Philharmonic Orchestra and a host of international soloists to perform the Bach Magnificat at that year's Festival.

Initially apprehensive of dealing with the great German conductor and his entourage of staff, Oldham found Karajan to be astonished by the EFC's achievements: 'Karajan told me, in his fractured English, "I would like to take you me with." The following day he gave a press conference at which he declared: "I made more progress with this choir in one hour than I make with most choirs in two weeks. This is one of the three great choirs of Europe."'

It was in 1969 that what began life as the Scottish Festival Chorus became the Edinburgh Festival Chorus – not without murmurings of dissent from the Chorus ranks, although it was soon accepted that it would always be 'Edinburgh's Festival Chorus' to the esteemed international orchestras and conductors the singers would work with. And down the years, the EFC has indeed performed with many of the greatest classical musicians of our times, in concerts memorable not just for the exceptional quality of their music making.

A 1975 performance of Beethoven's 'Choral' Symphony in Paris' Place de la Concorde, with the Orchestre de Paris conducted by Daniel Barenboim, had to be curtailed due to torrential rain. The EFC sang Handel's *Israel in Egypt* on a rock in Eilat in 1982, and Zimmermann's highly moving *Requiem für einen jungen Dichter* (Requiem for

a Young Poet) under Michael Gielen on a six-concert tour across Europe in 1995. And it has also found itself caught up in history. The EFC gave a special memorial concert for the victims of the Lockerbie bombing in 1989, conducted by John Mauceri, who had narrowly missed being on Pan Am flight 103 himself. EFC singers gave an emotionally charged performance of the Mozart Requiem in 1991, singing with an anxious Leningrad Philharmonic Orchestra and conductor Yuri Temirkanov on the same day that eight Soviet leaders staged a coup in Moscow, imprisoning president Mikhail Gorbachev and putting the future of his democratic reforms in question.

In its 50 years of existence, the Edinburgh Festival Chorus has given hundreds of exceptional performances, worked with some of the world's most influential musicians, and formed a vital connection between the city, the Festival and the international musical community. It's no wonder that former Festival Director Peter Diamand called the EFC 'Scotland's greatest indigenous contribution to the Edinburgh Festival.' And in the words of Lord Harewood, the Festival Director who co-founded it: 'It is rather agreeable to think from that small acorn planted, with much optimism, in 1964–5 has grown the mighty oak of today.' ∎

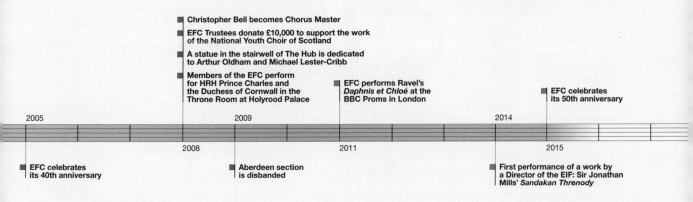

Christopher Bell becomes Chorus Master

EFC Trustees donate £10,000 to support the work of the National Youth Choir of Scotland

A statue in the stairwell of The Hub is dedicated to Arthur Oldham and Michael Lester-Cribb

Members of the EFC perform for HRH Prince Charles and the Duchess of Cornwall in the Throne Room at Holyrood Palace

EFC performs Ravel's *Daphnis et Chloé* at the BBC Proms in London

EFC celebrates its 50th anniversary

2005

2009

2014

2008

2011

2015

EFC celebrates its 40th anniversary

Aberdeen section is disbanded

First performance of a work by a Director of the EIF: Sir Jonathan Mills' *Sandakan Threnody*

Founding father

The Edinburgh Festival Chorus wouldn't be what it is today without the avuncular figure of its original Chorus Master, Arthur Oldham. Kate Molleson celebrates the man who, despite personal difficulties, set the EFC's lofty standards right from the start

Founder, twice Chorus Master, no individual has contributed more to the Edinburgh Festival Chorus than Arthur Oldham. His musicality is etched into the sound and ethos of the EFC, and his burly character is still vivid in the memories of long-standing members.

The adjective that comes up time and again from those who knew Oldham during his EFC days is 'avuncular'. With his thick black beard (snowy white in later life), gravelly cockney voice, wry humour, appetite for mild subversion and healthy suspicion of academic orthodoxy, he treated his singers well – at least in

> *Oldham was a man of strong values, conscious of his own humble origins*

part because he knew he got the best results by (in his words) being nice to people. EFC singers remember a bright spark who could be a little intimidating – 'He called himself a benign dictator,' remembers EFC alto Catriona McDonald – but who always gave his all to his Chorus.

Around the turn of the millennium, Oldham wrote a brief but candid memoir – *Living with Voices* – in which he discusses the egalitarian potential of amateur choruses. 'The fact that one is a managing director of a large industrial enterprise (and we have quite a few, along with doctors, schoolteachers, secretaries, journalists – even, at one time, a professional cyclist and a man who earned his living by sweeping the platforms of the Metro) counts for little once rehearsals get underway,' he wrote. This point clearly mattered to him a great deal. Oldham was a man of strong values, conscious of his own humble origins and of the early opportunities afforded

to him by a handful of unsnobby individuals.

Oldham founded three choruses – the Scottish Festival Chorus/EFC in 1965, the Chorus of the Orchestre de Paris in 1976, and the Chorus of the Concertgebouw Orchestra in 1980 – and worked closely with several high-profile others. His commitment was always to amateur singers, whose straight-up passion he found invigorating. He never considered the term 'amateur' a euphemism for rough quality: he expected the best from the EFC, and if he didn't get it, he made his disappointment plain to all.

There were two halves to Oldham's life, clearly separated by a nervous breakdown and his subsequent adoption of Catholic faith. Born in London in 1926, he had a natural gift for singing and was a good boy soprano. His mother turned down an invitation for him to join Southwark Cathedral Choir because she

considered music a shaky profession. Instead, she earmarked the young Arthur as a civil servant. He was determined, though, and taught himself to play piano. From the age of 11 he was offered free lessons by various musicians who recognised his talents.

Oldham's childhood wasn't easy. The family didn't have much money, his father died when he was 12, and his mother committed suicide when he was 14. He spent his adolescence with an adoptive family (he couldn't stand their enthusiastic amateur music making and would escape to the local church to bash moodily through Grieg's Piano Concerto whenever he could). A headteacher encouraged him to compose by assigning short pieces instead of corporal punishment. A history teacher took him to his first Promenade Concert when he was 15, and a music teacher submitted his work to the Royal College of Music, which awarded him a scholarship. ➡

Arthur Oldham with Daniel Barenboim in 1974

Courtesy Valerie Bryan

He found the RCM disappointing. He studied organ but hated it, then timpani and enjoyed it. He described his composition teacher Herbert Howells as 'a vain little man who would constantly refer me to his own works as an example of how music should be written'. Still, he never lacked ambition. He discovered the music of Benjamin Britten at a college concert and promptly introduced himself to the composer. He requested lessons; Britten didn't formally teach but did believe in apprenticeships, and invited Oldham to Suffolk to help with an opera. 'It turned out to

Perched on high: Oldham in a typical conducting position

be *Peter Grimes*,' Oldham later noted with bemusement. The mentoring continued for several years, not without its tensions, but Oldham revered the elder composer to the end.

His first official commission as a composer was a score for the Ballet Rambert, whose Music Director he became at just 19. After quitting college, he earned a stipend as proofreader for Boosey and Hawkes and he composed profusely. He wrote song cycles and small-scale orchestral works, and he had scores premiered at several Aldeburgh Festivals. Britten asked him to contribute to a set of variations on 'Sellinger's Round' alongside Michael Tippett, Lennox Berkeley, Humphrey Searle and William Walton. He felt enormous pressure and ended up taking on too much. In just three months of 1952 he wrote an opera for the English Opera Group (*Love in a Village*), a song cycle for Peter Pears and ballet score for Covent Garden. The stress eventually caused a breakdown, mental and physical, so severe that he lost the ability to discern musical pitch.

At the depths of his depression, Oldham decided to become a Catholic, and for a time he lived at the Dominican Priory in Hampstead. After

a while he was able to return to music (or music returned to him) and he took a post as Choir Master at St Mary's Metropolitan Cathedral in Edinburgh. This move to Scotland was, he would later say, the best decision he ever made. Scotland is where he met his first wife, Eileen, and where his children were born. Scotland is where he became one of the 20th century's great choir masters.

But when he arrived he felt lonely: he didn't know anyone, and his choristers at St Mary's wouldn't socialise with him. To win them over, he devoted his attention to early Scottish polyphony, particularly the works of Robert Carver, and the Choir soon gained a reputation. Carlo Maria Giulini made a point of attending Mass at St Mary's when he was conducting in Edinburgh.

Oldham established the EFC at the request of Lord Harewood and Alexander Gibson. For its 1965 inaugural performance of Mahler's Eighth Symphony, he gathered 200 adults and almost 100 boys (among them the young Donald Runnicles).

Legendary performances followed: Stravinsky's *Symphony of Psalms* with Claudio Abbado; Brahms' *Ein deutsches Requiem* with Daniel Barenboim; Verdi's Requiem and Beethoven's *Missa solemnis* with Giulini; Britten's *War Requiem* with Gibson. In 1992, Oldham began rehearsals of Schoenberg's staggeringly difficult opera *Moses and Aaron*. Such was the complexity of the work, Assistant Chorus Master Michael Lester-Cribb and EFC pianist Angela Livingstone took on extra coaching and rehearsal responsibilities to assist Oldham in training the Chorus.

EFC member Ivor Klayman describes Oldham's personality in the early days as a mixture of the fierce and the loveable. 'His background was working with children at St Mary's, and he occasionally treated us like children too. Some members

Oldham at a 1994 ceremony in Edinburgh's City Chambers to mark his final season as EFC Chorus Master

didn't like it, some put up with it, and others like myself – who had never sung in another choir – didn't know any different.' Oldham was prone to telling tangential stories in rehearsal but liked discipline from his choristers, and he always began with his infamous warm-up of singing 'Popocatepetl' up and down the scale. The results were plainly worth it: the Chorus sang with accuracy, full tone, a formidable *forte* whisper and that classic EFC 'wall of sound'.

Oldham was never pretentious and he loathed that quality in others (Bernstein was never a favourite). Annie, his second wife, describes his relationship with conductors as 'absolutely equal. When he talked about music with Karajan, Giulini, Barenboim, whoever, there was no barrier.' Catriona McDonald recalls Oldham in rehearsal, galloping through the stalls to the foot of the Usher Hall stage in order to offer his opinion up to whichever conductor happened to be on stage. 'Eventually somebody got him a ladder,' she says.

Oldham and remaining founder members of the Scottish Festival Chorus at his final EFC concert, 1994

Sean Hudson

Courtesy Tori Graham

Le Mac Laren nouveau est arrivé!

1994 cartoon celebrating Oldham's arrival in Burgundy by one of Oldham's French choir members

For the EFC's tenth anniversary Oldham composed *Psalms in Time of War*, a work designed to show off the best of the singers. It was premiered in 1977 with Thomas Allen and the Scottish National Orchestra under Gibson, and though Oldham himself wasn't fully pleased with it ('too bombastic; too many crashy cymbals'), many in the Chorus recall it fondly.

Meanwhile, his career grew and grew. He became Chorus Master of Scottish Opera in 1964, three years after the company was formed; he took on the Chorus of the London Symphony Orchestra in 1969, working alongside Colin Davis and André Previn. At Barenboim's invitation he went to Paris to form a new Chorus for the Orchestre de Paris in 1976; at Bernard Haitink's invitation he formed a new Chorus for the Concertgebouw Orchestra in 1980.

But there was always, according to Annie Oldham, a 'gravitational pull' towards Edinburgh. For the 1987 Festival he returned to the EFC to become its Chorus Master for the

second time. 'He wasn't quite the same when he came back,' admits Klayman. 'He wasn't quite as demanding. He would let things slip that he wouldn't have previously. He once said that he liked Scots because we had discipline and passion. In London they had passion but no discipline, he said; in Amsterdam discipline but no passion. And in France? Apparently neither!'

Eventually the weekly commutes between Edinburgh and Paris became too exhausting, and in 1994 Oldham resigned from the EFC for the second and last time. Mahler's Eighth Symphony was on the bill of his final Festival (conducted, fittingly, by the now renowned Donald Runnicles).

Towards the end of his life, Oldham spent as much time as possible at his old farmhouse in Burgundy. He tended not to tell his neighbours there that he was a musician; he preferred to talk about the flowers and vegetables he grew in his garden. He died in 2003, aged 78. Without him, the EFC would probably have still come into existence, but it would not be the Chorus it is today. ■

On the road

Tours outside Scotland have played an important role in the Edinburgh Festival Chorus' activities since its early days. Kathy Crawford Hay looks back on some of the highlights

Once the Edinburgh Festival Chorus had established its integral role in the Edinburgh International Festival, invitations started to arrive for the Chorus to perform in concerts outside Scotland. Since the early 1970s, there have been performances in England – in Ely Cathedral and London's Royal Festival Hall and Royal Albert Hall (including five at the BBC Proms, most recently in 2010 and 2011) – as well as in Austria, France, Germany and Israel.

Paris has been the most frequently visited city, the most memorable of its nine EFC performances being an outdoor concert in 1975 at the Place de la Concorde in front of 100,000 Parisians. Despite torrential rain and with the help of tarpaulins provided by the Paris fire brigade – all of which later earnt the event the nickname 'Splash de la Concorde' – the EFC performed the final movement of Beethoven's 'Choral' Symphony with the Orchestre de Paris, conducted by Daniel Barenboim. There were also concerts in Rouen and Paris with Yuri Temirkanov, in Lyon and La Côte-St-André with John Eliot Gardiner, and in Paris with James Conlon.

At Christmas and New Year 1981–2, the EFC was joined by members of the Scottish National Orchestra Chorus and the John Currie Singers to perform for three nights in Jerusalem.

Following performances of Handel's *Israel in Egypt*, Walton's *Belshazzar's Feast* and Berlioz's *Grande messe des morts*, the EFC was bussed 370km through the Negev Desert to take part in an extraordinary televised broadcast on top of a rock in Eilat. Orchestra, singers and soloists scrambled up cliff paths and, in full evening dress in uncomfortable heat, performed *Israel in Egypt* again, watched by a curious audience who were similarly perched on adjacent cliffs. The performers were tightly packed close to the cliff edge with little room to move, and even less by way of cooling drinks. There followed a rather surreal picnic on the beach below, with choristers in full evening dress paddling in the Red Sea and eating what was left of their kibbutz breakfast.

Munich's Lukaskirche was the venue for a 1984 performance of Fauré's Requiem and Parry's *Blest Pair of Sirens*, conducted by John Currie, part of a 30th anniversary celebration of the twinning of the city with Edinburgh. This trip coincided with the Munich Oktoberfest, and many who were there still recall outsinging everyone else in the city's main bierkeller.

Two years after Frank Dunlop took over as Festival Director, the EFC took part in three astonishing staged performances in Edinburgh of Weber's *Oberon* – part opera, part pantomime,

The EFC visits Versailles as part of its rainy concert trip to Paris in 1975

Courtesy David Bonnar

with costumes, mermaids, soloists on specially built discs set above the orchestra, and the EFC members seated behind a black gauze screen, wearing black polo-neck jumpers so

> *Orchestra, singers and soloists scrambled up cliff paths and, in full evening dress, performed 'Israel in Egypt'*

that only their faces were visible. This magical production then travelled to Frankfurt's Alte Oper for two further performances, and it was there that the back row of the Chorus managed to upend itself and disappear off the platform, accompanied by stifled laughter from the rest of the singers – all during a televised broadcast.

But it was in 1995 that the EFC took part in one of its most ambitious international tours. Determined to revive and perform Bernd Alois Zimmermann's dramatic *Requiem for a Young Poet* to mark 50 years since the liberation of Europe from fascism, conductor Michael Gielen worked with the management of South-West German Radio, Baden-Baden, to put together a series of performances of the enormous work in Salzburg, Cologne, Berlin, Paris and Edinburgh, in a co-production between the Edinburgh International Festival, Salzburg Festival, Festival d'Automne Paris and Berlin Festwochen, in collaboration with Kölner Rundfunk and the SWF Symphony Orchestra Baden-Baden.

The performances involved more than 300 singers, a 70-strong orchestra (minus violins and violas), soloists, synchronised four-track tapes and a jazz band. The piece included

fragments of songs from Wagner and the Beatles, as well as speeches by Hitler, Churchill and Mussolini. There were six concerts in total, with a commercial recording made in Salzburg and a television documentary filmed by WDR in Cologne.

All the planning was in place when David Jones took over as Chorus Master in 1995. Rehearsals started in January that year with 80 EFC members. In March the Chorus spent five days in Salzburg, meeting and rehearsing with the other choirs, as well as making the commercial recording and giving a performance of the Requiem in the Grosses Festspielhaus. They then travelled to Germany for a performance in

Berlin's Konzerthaus, and in August everyone returned to Salzburg for a second concert there, later travelling to Edinburgh for a Festival performance, then to Paris and finally to Cologne in September. David Jones said: 'This piece, and the tour, demonstrated the very best qualities of the EFC – committed and professional in rehearsal and always giving everything they had to the performance. The Zimmermann Requiem is a daunting challenge and the EFC took it, as they have so much other repertoire, in their stride.' This extraordinary, thought-provoking concert tour was well received by audiences – with tears (from the older generation) and cheers (from younger listeners) in equal measure. ∎

Israel in Egypt on a rock in Eilat, 1982

Courtesy David Arulanantham

In rehearsal at the BBC Proms, 2010: the Edinburgh Festival Chorus joins the RSNO Junior Chorus, BBC Scottish Symphony Orchestra, conductor Donald Runnicles and mezzo soprano Karen Cargill

Behind the scenes at the Edinburgh Festival Chorus' 1982 Eilat performance (left) and at Edinburgh rehearsals and concerts (right)

The grit and the glamour

It takes talent and commitment to make it through the rigorous audition process and perform with one of the UK's finest choruses. From waiting on cold stone steps to singing for some of the world's greatest conductors, Kathy Crawford Hay reveals what the public never sees

Peter Sandground

Why do I – or any of us – sing in the Edinburgh Festival Chorus? What is the reason for spending almost all of August sitting on uncomfortable wooden seats for hours, abandoning family and work? It is quite simply that, as an amateur singer, I want to perform at a professional level and sing a huge and varied range of choral works and concert performances of operas.

The EFC is not just another amateur choir – far from it. When work started on the recruitment of choral singers for the original Scottish Festival Chorus, the process was rigorous, demanding and thorough – and it remains so. Today, advertisements inviting people to audition appear in Festival programmes, leaflets are distributed, and those who are interested can also contact the Festival office through the EIF website. Chorus Master Christopher Bell will look for singers with experience, but not necessarily for perfect sight-readers or those with huge voices. He will blend the sound, and place those who are not brilliant at reading music alongside others with more experience.

My first audition took place in 1983 with Chorus Master John Currie, in the lecture theatre of the Western General Hospital, the main rehearsal venue for the EFC at that time. Now that our home is The Hub, auditions take place in that building's Main Hall or Dunard Library, or at the Music Box in Edinburgh College's Sighthill Campus, a state-of-the-art music and performing arts centre. Auditions take the form of sight-singing, a range test, a section from a specified choral work, and a formal audition piece. They are arranged to a strict timetable. When you arrive, there will be four or five folk waiting with very concentrated expressions on their faces. Not much talk, even among friends. And then in you go, meet the pianist and Chorus Master, and do your best. I cannot think of anything more

stressful than going through the EFC audition process. And it doesn't just happen once – we are re-auditioned on a regular basis. At the end of the audition there is no comment from the Chorus Master – you just have to wait for the letter to arrive a few days later from the Chorus Manager.

Once welcomed in, we are expected to attend every rehearsal, and EFC members sign in at the start of each

> *We are fortunate to have first-class professional language coaches who painstakingly guide us through non-English works*

session. The Chorus Manager keeps an eye on absentees: the office will, of course, deal sympathetically with personal issues, but missing too many rehearsals can be a problem as we work so fast that it would be difficult to catch up if you were not there.

Rehearsals take place from October to June in preparation for August. At first it seemed strange to me that the EFC was given the whole of July off. Why not power on into August? The pattern has been the same for years, and the plan is quite clear. Everything should be concert-perfect by June. You can then relax, take a holiday, and come back ready in the first week of August, good to go.

The EFC rehearses on Tuesday evenings, working hard for two and a half hours, with a short tea break in the middle. (Thank goodness for the cuppa, which is cheerfully served up by two EFC stalwarts, Susan and Malcolm Crosby, who have volunteered to do this very necessary task for years.) The Chorus

Master works on one piece of music at a time, puts it to bed after four or so rehearsals, then starts the next one. No chat, concentrate with pencil and eraser in hand, as corrections land like rapid fire. There are also usually around five weekend rehearsals throughout the year when all the works being performed are reviewed. When a standard work that the EFC has performed before is scheduled, the Chorus Master checks to see how many people are singing it for the first time.

If the standard work has not been performed for a while, everyone is expected to do some homework so that when Tuesday-night rehearsals come round, they are not held back by note-bashing. (When John Currie was Chorus Master, new members to the EFC joined a training choir for the first year before taking part in any concert performance.) Come August, everyone is expected to attend every rehearsal. It is obligatory to attend the conductor's piano rehearsal: non-attendance would probably mean that that person would not be allowed to sing in the concert.

The EFC sings an astonishing range of works in a dozen different languages, from Hebrew to French, Slavic languages to German. We are fortunate to have first-class professional language coaches who painstakingly guide us through non-English works. The coach (usually also a musician) will say a short phrase, which the EFC then repeats. During just one rehearsal, we work through the whole score, short phrases at a time. There will also be printed pronunciation notes and on occasion, a complete score might be specially produced for the EFC, with phonetics in place. Each person is expected to annotate their own score as we go along. Closer to the performance, the language coach returns to check on progress and correct any problems, and again, we're expected to do our homework.

The Usher Hall is the principal concert venue for the majority of our performances. It's a grand edifice with a beautiful interior and – mostly – very comfortable seats for the audience. For choristers, however, it's a rather different story. The seats in the organ gallery are all square, straight-backed and wooden, with limited legroom – not so appealing when performing, say, a four-hour Wagner opera. And with the EFC numbering anything from 110 to

Meeting the conductor is usually a cheerful affair with anecdotes and a few jokes

180, depending on the work being presented, backstage can be less than luxurious too. There are only a handful of small dressing rooms and only a few seats available. We arrive already wearing our concert clothes, and there is much sitting around in the stairwell on cold stone steps, or maybe sharing a coffee with colleagues in a nearby café before it is time to line up in serried ranks and walk onto the platform. Choristers tend not to eat a meal before a concert, and after the performance, many race to nearby restaurants to share food, wine and our own critique of what just took place in the concert hall.

The same formula of rehearsal and performance generally applies to each August concert – which, by the way, usually only happens once in a Festival. In other words, we have only one chance to get it right! We meet the conductor for the first time two or three days before the concert, for his (or rarely her) one and only piano rehearsal with just the EFC. It's usually a cheerful affair with anecdotes, background stories and

a few jokes. He or she will listen to the whole piece and then reprise sections to refine phrases or note lengths. On the day after the conductor's piano rehearsal, it's time to meet the soloists and orchestra for one or maybe two general rehearsals, which take place in the Usher Hall, Glasgow City Halls, Glasgow Royal Concert Hall or Henry Wood Hall (home to the Royal Scottish National Orchestra in Glasgow), depending on which orchestra is performing. The EFC is always keen to hear how the piece comes together, not least since we often work with choral scores which are abbreviated versions of the work, meaning huge swathes are sometimes unheard by the Chorus until the tutti rehearsal. Then the general rehearsal follows on the day of the concert, in either the morning or early afternoon, and finally the concert in the evening.

Taking part in EIF concerts is quite an undertaking, given than the EFC is asked to perform four, five or six times in August. And with trips abroad or visits to the BBC Proms at London's Royal Albert Hall, no wonder we appreciate our partners and families: without their understanding and support, it would be a very difficult task for us all. For many years, the EFC had no idea what lay ahead when the end of the Festival approached, since the following year's offerings were kept firmly under wraps. Similarly,

Thank goodness for the tea-break cuppa, cheerfully served up by two EFC stalwarts

the Festival office would have no idea whether EFC members would return – there was no contract, and no guaranteed commitment. But now, and usually before our final concert, we are delighted when the Festival Director gives us a flavour of what's in store the following year, so that we can look forward to the arrival of the letter inviting us to return to the Chorus.

The EFC is made up of accountants, teachers, nurses, sales and marketing experts, solicitors, fundraisers, charity workers, civil engineers, students, ministers, writers, musicians and doctors. Many have sung with the Chorus for more than 30 years; for some it will be their first year; and others may have taken part in a dozen or so Festivals. All are there for one reason – to sing with one of the finest choirs in the UK. And since its debut in 1965, the EFC has remained the most truly indigenous and only continuous performing body of Edinburgh's magnificent International Festival. ∎

Backstage pre-concert relaxation

Vital cuppa suppliers: Susan and Malcolm Crosby

Clark James

Master of the voices

Energetic, ambitious and a stickler for exceptional standards, the EFC's Chorus Master Christopher Bell is nevertheless a rare presence on the concert platform. Kate Molleson discovers a man driven by an innate passion for working with singers

➡

Christopher Bell knows his choirs. Over the past three decades he has worked with professional singers and amateurs, young voices and veterans, chamber-sized ensembles and massed symphonic choirs. He has a parallel career in orchestral conducting, partially for the added perspective it gives him on symphonic choral repertoire. But there's no doubt in his mind which of these set-ups generates the highest musical voltage. 'The thrill of a volunteer chorus singing with a visiting international orchestra, a great maestro and world-class soloists? That creates a kind of electricity that you can't necessarily achieve with professional

> **'I discovered I had a natural ability to work with volunteers and youth choirs, to find ways of fixing things'**

choirs,' he says. 'A large volunteer chorus can harness something quite natural. It's the desire in us all to be part of something bigger and better than ourselves.'

Bell has been an invigorating force with the Edinburgh Festival Chorus. The dynamism it produces under his watch can be monumental, as shown in recent performances of Mahler's Second Symphony with Mariss Jansons, Mahler's Eighth with Donald Runnicles, Prokofiev's *Alexander Nevsky* with Valery Gergiev, and many others. Today's EFC is energetic, versatile and committed. Bell believes that a successful concert is all about partnership: between chorus and chorus master, between chorus and orchestra, between musicians and conductor, between stage and

audience. And he also believes in due recognition.

'A son travels through life hoping that one day his father will tell him that he's been a good son. What the son doesn't realise is that the father travels through life hoping that the son will tell him he's been a good father. Jollying a chorus along, finding the right alchemy, keeping them entertained with enough background stories so that it's interesting but not too many so that it's boring... There's a lot of input I give to the EFC to get them where they need to be for a concert. Every single note the Chorus sings has had attention from me. The one presence who cannot be taken away but is hardly visible on stage is the Chorus Master.'

But there's no person more recognisable in Scotland's choral world than Bell. He was Chorus Master of the Royal Scottish National Orchestra Chorus from 1989 to 2002; he has run

the RSNO Junior Chorus since 1994; he founded the National Youth Choir of Scotland in 1996 and remains its Artistic Director; and he has been EFC Chorus Master since the 2008 Festival. Through NYCoS, Bell's impact on youth singing in Scotland has been immeasurable, and he has developed future singers for choruses across the country. He's a spry man in his early 50s, but his life hasn't been without its hurdles – he suffered a brain tumour in 2008 – although today his energy and ambition seem inexhaustible.

Bell describes growing up in a Belfast 'patrolled by the soldiers and dark angst'. His father was a clergyman and he was a choirboy from the age of 11. He was always interested in buildings – he wanted to study architecture as a boy – but a life in music was, he says, inevitable. He arrived in Edinburgh in 1979 as an undergraduate organist and oboist (slicing off the top of a finger in a wood planer in 1986 would cause ➡

An invigorating force: Bell in action

Clark James

A history of influential leaders

Peter Somerford looks back at the EFC's eminent Chorus Masters since its founding in 1965

Arthur Oldham

In its 50 years, the Edinburgh Festival Chorus has had only four Chorus Masters, the length of their tenures evidence both of their loyalty and commitment to the EFC, and of the pride and affection the Chorus inspires in its leaders. The original Chorus Master was Arthur Oldham, who remained in the post until 1977, and then returned for a second stint from 1987 to 1994.

Between 1977 and 1986, the Chorus Master was John Currie. He was Director of the Scottish National Orchestra Chorus and had also founded his own chamber choir, the John Currie Singers. He signalled his intent to achieve universally high vocal standards in the EFC by launching a training choir that would meet before rehearsals.

EFC member Dorothy Fairweather remembers: 'John was very good at illustrating how he wanted us to sing, and he was protective of our voices. He also enjoyed explaining the historical context of the music.'

After Oldham's final season as Chorus Master, David Jones took over ahead of the 1995 Festival, bringing extensive operatic and orchestral conducting experience. 'He was always thorough in rehearsals, well prepared, and very good on details,' says Fairweather. 'In his first year, he had to prepare a huge, challenging work by Bernd Alois Zimmermann, the *Requiem for a Young Poet*. It was completely different to anything most of us had sung before, and it was David's tenacity that helped get us through this very difficult work.'

'It was incredibly difficult music,' says Jones himself, 'but I'd had a lot of experience of very difficult orchestral music, so I was able to put it together with confidence. The EFC joined forces with choruses from Cologne,

Stuttgart and Bratislava for performances across Europe as well as a commercial recording and TV documentary, so it was an exciting project to be involved in at the start of my tenure.'

The current Chorus Master, Christopher Bell, started in the post for the 2008 Festival. Chorus member Peter Cannell describes Bell as 'a wonderful musician with a fantastic ear, who knows how to get the best from voices'. He adds: 'Christopher is a true advocate for the EFC, he inspires people, and he is a superb technician.'

All four Chorus Masters have been supported by assistants, the longest-serving of whom was

Michael Lester-Cribb, Assistant Chorus Master and the main rehearsal pianist from 1965 to 2006. The Aberdeen section of the chorus had a number of Assistant Chorus Masters, beginning with Tom Devine, who was appointed to assist Arthur Oldham. Devine ran the section until 1977, and then the job passed through John Hearne to Roger Williams, and then to Steve Farrand. After a four-year hiatus when the Aberdeen section was cut from the EFC set-up, pianist Bobby Howie returned in 1993 to direct the singers from the piano until 2005. Gordon Jack then took over for the last four years until the Aberdeen section was disbanded in 2009. ∎

John Currie

David Jones

problems for the latter role) and went on to do a Master's degree on the history of instruments and north German organ music.

As he began his Master's, Bell was approached by the music department's Director of Studies. 'The university choir needs a conductor,' he was informed. 'Would you do it?' Bell said no: he couldn't fathom conducting a non-auditioned ensemble. A few weeks later he was contacted again by the Director of Studies and told that he 'would do the job as well as anyone else'. Bell laughs at the memory. 'What a ringing endorsement to launch my career!'

He describes his very first rehearsal as 'utterly clueless'. But the second? 'I got this energy. Maybe it was the link with my father and his love of preaching to people. Maybe it was the opportunity to show leadership. I discovered I had a natural ability to work with volunteers and youth choirs, to find ways of fixing things. I love it when something isn't working – I can rip it apart, fix the intonation, put it back together again. The singers feel better; I feel better. Beautiful.'

The fix-it skills accumulated over time. Bell refers to his nearly two decades of work with NYCoS as 'the single most beneficial thing' for his own musical development. The young singers are offered professional coaching, through which Bell too has gleaned invaluable technical tips. He twice applied for the EFC job and was twice turned down, but eventually he was successful. 'I was sitting in my apartment in Chicago' – he is

Bell and the EFC in rehearsal at The Hub

Chorus Director of the city's Grant Park Music Festival – 'and the phone rang. A voice from Edinburgh said: "We want to know whether you'd like to come on board." I held the phone still for a moment and didn't speak.

> ### 'The one presence who cannot be taken away but is hardly visible on stage is the Chorus Master'

This was the job I'd been waiting for.' He acknowledges that only then was he finally ready: thanks to his work with NYCoS and a growing career as an orchestral conductor, his ear was now honed enough and his technical toolkit well enough equipped.

Bell knows exactly what he's looking for in an EFC vocal audition. 'What is paramount isn't big voices or operatic voices, but voices that can work together to create a real line. The results from volunteer singers can be staggeringly good.' He's keen to accommodate the everyday working lives of his members, aware that the traditional rehearsal format isn't always conducive to contemporary lifestyles.

'Nowadays people have portfolio careers,' he says. 'They need to earn a living. Things have changed quite dramatically since what might be described as the heyday of choral team spirit, when every member turned up for every single rehearsal or else. Modern life just doesn't work like that. But the musical standards? There is never any compromise there, and I think the concerts speak for themselves.' ∎

Where it all happens

Kathy Crawford Hay reflects on the spaces that have housed the Edinburgh Festival Chorus – for rehearsals and performances – throughout its history

The Edinburgh Festival Chorus in performance in the Usher Hall, 2002

A hospital lecture theatre, a gloomy church, a school assembly hall, the confines of a theatre stage or the basement of a cinema – all these and more have, over the years, provided the many rehearsal venues for the Edinburgh Festival Chorus. The very first rehearsals for the Chorus' inaugural 1965 concert were held in the basement of Poole's Synod Hall Cinema (subsequently the site of Edinburgh's infamous 'hole in the ground', which eventually became the elegant Saltire Court). Long-standing EFC member John Anderton recalls: 'The experience of singing in the basement of a cinema was somewhat surreal. Mahler's Eighth Symphony has many passages calling for fortissimo singing and our conductor Arthur Oldham did his utmost to encourage us to "lift the roof off". This, of course, caused great annoyance to the cinema proprietors, whose clients were somewhat put out by the repeated loud blasts of "Veni Creator Spiritus" as they tried to enjoy the less uplifting creations being shown on the large screen. "Quiet, quiet!" hissed the cinema usherettes as they rushed ➔

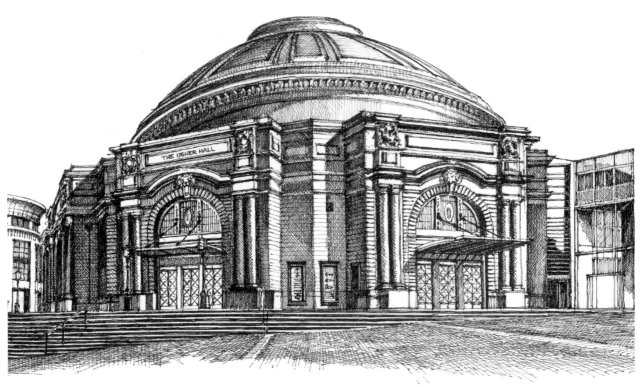

Edinburgh's Usher Hall in a 2014 drawing by Ian Stuart Campbell, commissioned by the EFC Trustees

into the room, but Arthur continued to encourage us to sing "loud, loud".'

Happily, the principal rehearsal venue for the EFC is now the Main Hall at The Hub, the magnificent gothic building that stands at the top of the Lawnmarket close to Castlehill, its serrated spire visible for miles. The Hub is the headquarters of the Edinburgh International Festival, which also moved from cramped offices elsewhere in the city to this reworked, multifunctional structure. The building originally opened in the 1840s as a General Assembly Hall for the Church of Scotland, and its Main Hall, with its light wood panelling and zany colour scheme, is a perfect venue for EFC rehearsals, which are held each Tuesday evening and on a handful of weekends throughout the year.

A key element of any rehearsal is a good piano, and The Hub is also home to a very fine Bösendorfer grand that was jointly purchased by the EIF and the EFC Trustees in 2004. It bears a pair of brass plaques remembering the two men who formed the EFC so many years ago, Michael Lester-Cribb and Arthur Oldham.

The majority of EFC concerts are held in the equally magnificent Usher Hall, renowned for its superb acoustics. In 1896, Andrew Usher, a whisky distiller, donated £100,000 for the building of a concert hall. The work eventually began in 1911, and the Hall opened in 1914. There is a huge difference between singing in a good rehearsal venue, even The Hub, and singing in the Usher Hall, and it is noticeable that conductors may urge us to give more during a rehearsal at The Hub, only to be taken aback by the volume of sound that comes at them from the Usher Hall platform.

The EFC has also given performances in many well-known theatres and concert halls throughout Europe, including the Grosses Festspielhaus in Salzburg, the Alte Oper Frankfurt, Paris' Châtelet Theatre, Cologne's Philharmonie Hall, Berlin's Konzerthaus and the Lukaskirche, Munich. But they and even London's mighty Royal Albert Hall struggle to match the acoustics of Edinburgh's Usher Hall, one of the world's finest concert venues. ∎

A keyboard orchestra

Edinburgh Festival Chorus pianist Stuart Hope reveals to Peter Somerford the challenges and rewards of conveying an orchestral score to 130 singers

There's a particular art to accompanying a chorus. According to Stuart Hope, the Edinburgh Festival Chorus' rehearsal pianist since 2013, it all comes down to playing what the singers need to hear, rather than the notes on the page. 'When you accompany a solo singer, you play everything that's written in the score,' he explains. 'But with a Chorus, a lot of the time you're not actually playing what's written, because the score is either made up for a conductor and has too many notes in it, or it doesn't have specific notes that the Chorus will hear from the orchestra.' This means that Hope effectively has to make up his own version of what the orchestra would be doing, making modifications during the rehearsal process to ensure that the singers always hear what they need to hear.

How did Hope learn this discipline? 'I've never trained to do it, but I've played for choirs since I was 12. I've picked up the skills along the way, watching others do the job, and learning how to do it myself.' Hope studied music at Edinburgh University and has been freelancing as a pianist ever since. He's worked with the

Scottish Chamber Orchestra Chorus for nearly 20 years, he accompanied the Royal Scottish National Orchestra Chorus for ten years, and has been involved with the National Youth Choir of Scotland since its inception in 1996. It was his long-time colleague Christopher Bell, Chorus Master of the Edinburgh Festival Chorus and NYCoS Artistic Director, who brought him in as the EFC's pianist during the 2013–14 season.

Hope isn't exclusively a choral pianist. He accompanies soloists too, but says there is nothing quite like playing for a large chorus: 'I like the feeling of being in a room with lots of people singing at me. It's such a great noise!' But away from the visceral thrill of rehearsals, the job demands a great deal of technical preparation. A case in point is the work Hope did ahead of rehearsals for the 2014 Festival performance of Janáček's *Glagolitic Mass*, a piece that he'd never played before. 'The score I received was a conductor's guide score,' he says, 'and there was no ➡

Playing what the singers need to hear: pianist Stuart Hope

Clark James

way that I would have been able to play all the notes in it.' In these circumstances, Hope listens carefully to a recording of the work, picks out the most prominent or essential elements, and then removes all the non-essential parts from his score. 'Then I have to work out a way to make what I hear in the orchestra happen from what's left on the page,' he says.

Reproducing an orchestral sound on the piano is a challenge in itself, but Hope has a range of techniques in his arsenal. 'For trumpets, I might accent the notes, or for violins, try to make a smoother sound. Timpani rolls are easy to replicate with a big wiggle of the left hand, and if there's a harp in the orchestra I can spread chords instead of just playing them as written. There are lots of little things a choral pianist can do to hint at what the orchestra will sound like.' Capturing huge variations in dynamics is also part of the fun, he says: 'You have to be able to do everything, from *pppp* up to *ffff*.' Having a decent instrument helps, of course, and Hope is full of praise for the big Bösendorfer he gets to play on for rehearsals in

The Hub: 'It's a great piano that can do everything I need it to do.'

The Chorus Master naturally feeds into the pianist's strategy of drawing out what the EFC needs to hear. 'I'll have discussions with Christopher,' says Hope, 'and he'll say if he wants something specific brought out at a certain point, or he might ask me to play something in rehearsal even though it won't be heard in the performance.' Hope adds that because he's known Bell for such a long time, their working relationship is characterised by an instinctive understanding. 'I know what he likes and how his rehearsals run,' says the pianist, 'and I know the sorts of passages he is going to fix before he fixes them.'

Bell deals with matters of musical interpretation, explains Hope, and will rehearse certain parts of a piece in a number of different ways so that the EFC is prepared for the conductor to start changing things at the final piano rehearsal prior to the performance. The start of that rehearsal is when Hope feels the most pressure. 'If it's a conductor I've not worked with before, I'll have no idea

what mood they're going to be in, and sometimes I won't know if I'll even be able to follow them,' he says. 'But on the whole, those rehearsals work out fine.'

One of the most pressurised moments for the singers – unsurprisingly – is their initial audition, where Hope will meet them for the first time. He doesn't know the repertoire in advance, and because of the range of abilities and musical interests among prospective Chorus members, he's confronted by a huge range of audition material. 'Some singers particularly enjoy solo singing, and will turn up with showpiece arias,' he says. 'Others, who are only

> *'Being in the rehearsal room and crashing around on the piano with 130 people singing their hearts out is just the best thing ever'*

choral singers, find it difficult to choose a solo work. We always advise them to sing something that they're comfortable with and that shows off their voice. It doesn't have to be big or grand.'

When he isn't working with choruses, Hope runs his own 15-voice choir, accompanies soloists, plays continuo for a number of groups, and teaches and arranges music. It's a packed portfolio career, but he says that playing for the EFC gives him a singular buzz. 'There's a special pay-off with this job. After all the huge amount of preparation that has to be done, actually being in the rehearsal room and crashing around on the piano with 130 people singing their hearts out is just the best thing ever.' ∎

Stuart Hope and Christopher Bell in rehearsal at The Hub

Stuart Armitt

A roll-call of eminent pianists

We look back over the illustrious history of the Edinburgh Festival Chorus pianists

Michael Lester-Cribb, pianist and Assistant Chorus Master 1965–2006

With three sections – in Edinburgh, Glasgow and Aberdeen – operating for substantial periods of its existence, the Edinburgh Festival Chorus has had many accompanists over the years. Chief among them, and longest-serving, was Michael Lester-Cribb. He was the main rehearsal pianist, as well as Assistant Chorus Master, from 1965 until his death in October 2006. He worked closely with Arthur Oldham in auditioning and forming the first Chorus for the performance of Mahler's gigantic Eighth Symphony that opened the 1965 Festival.

Lester-Cribb was by all accounts a brilliant sight-reader with an astonishing musical ear, and proved a highly sensitive and supportive choral accompanist. He was also a composer, like Oldham, and was Music Director at Edinburgh's Fettes College. He was his own accompanist when required to take rehearsals, and among his achievements as Assistant Chorus

Master was helping the EFC conquer the immensely challenging atonal world of Schoenberg's *Moses and Aaron* for the 1992 Festival.

Lester-Cribb also played the organ in EFC performances, including the Mahler Eighth Symphony in 1965. He later wrote in his unpublished autobiography: 'The greatest sense of power I have ever experienced was playing the first chord of that year's Festival on full organ and sensing the entire audience being rocketed out of their seats.'

In the same colourful yet self-effacing account, Lester-Cribb recalled some 'especially interesting, if sometimes nerve-racking events' during conductors' piano rehearsals. 'André Previn once leaned over while Oldham was conducting part of a rehearsal and asked: "Are you lost?" "Yes," answered the pianist, and Previn said, "So am I."' Lester-Cribb's widow Susan says that he loved the opportunities to work with conductors: 'He found the job thrilling because it brought him into contact with so many brilliant musicians.'

EFC pianist Sam Hutchings (left) and Aberdeen section pianist Bobbie Howie (right)

Following Lester-Cribb's death in 2006, Sam Hutchings became rehearsal pianist. He had the same role with the Royal Scottish National Orchestra Chorus and Junior Chorus, and worked alongside Christopher Bell at the National Youth Choir of Scotland. Hutchings was a youthful and talented presence in the Chorus family, but sadly died in 2012.

The roll call of pianists who accompanied the Glasgow section of the Chorus includes Jack Keaney and Ian Robertson, who is now Chorus Director at San Francisco Opera. Angela Livingstone was an accompanist for both the Glasgow and Edinburgh sections, and is presently Head of Opera, Vocal Performance and Choral Conducting at the Royal Welsh College of Music and Drama in Cardiff.

Bobbie Howie was a long-serving pianist for the Aberdeen section. He worked with Assistant Chorus Master Tom Devine from 1965 to 1977, shared piano duties for the next ten years with Drew Tulloch, and then directed the section from the piano from 1993 until 2005. EFC member David Arulanantham says of Howie: 'He was a brilliant pianist, as good as Michael Lester-Cribb, and he effectively kept the Aberdeen section going for a long time.' When Howie retired, Lesley Milne took over as pianist until 2009, when the Aberdeen section was disbanded. ∎

A singer's perspective

Eight Edinburgh Festival Chorus singers reveal why the ensemble is so special to them

Name David Arulanantham
Year joined 1971
Most memorable concert
Mahler's Second Symphony with Leonard Bernstein.
Motivation for being part of the EFC We are given an opportunity to work with top-class conductors and performers, and an insight into the way they work, rehearse and perform.
What do you find especially fulfilling about being part of the EFC?
This is the only activity where absolutely the best is demanded from one, without any compromise. This has been my addiction, far better than alcohol or other drugs. Living in Aberdeen for most of the last 40 years, travelling regularly to attend rehearsals and concerts in Edinburgh has been a struggle, but it's hugely rewarding when we sing in concerts to a full Usher Hall with some of the best musicians on the circuit. ■

Name Valerie Bryan
Year joined First in 1973–1975, then again in 2011
Most memorable concert
First time: Fauré's Requiem in Paris, January 1974. Second time: Beethoven's Ninth in the Usher Hall in November 2014.
Motivation for being part of the EFC Being a member of the EFC in my twenties had a huge impact. Working at such a high, demanding, professional level, singing in performances alongside musical heroes was almost beyond belief. The inspiration stayed with me, and has pervaded my musical and teaching life.
What do you find especially fulfilling about being part of the EFC?
The EFC is absolutely unique! I love the music, the sound, the energy, the buzz, the camaraderie and the choral discipline; I love the expectation that we all strive, literally, for perfection. ■

Name Peter Cannell
Year joined 1981
Most memorable concert
The Verdi Requiem in 1982, conducted by Claudio Abbado with the London Symphony Orchestra.
Motivation for being part of the EFC My main motivation is to be part of an enduring tradition of performance on the top-class professional musical stage that makes a significant contribution not only to the artistic life of Edinburgh, but also far beyond. It is a challenge.
What do you find especially fulfilling about being part of the EFC? The challenge of performance; the continual amazement at how so many voices can sound as one coherent body; the appreciation of conductors and orchestras; the roar of the audience; being a performer in the world-famous Edinburgh International Festival; and simply being part of it! ■

Name Liliana Currie
Year joined 2005
Most memorable concert
Wagner's *Die Meistersinger von Nürnberg* in 2006, as it was the first year I performed with the EFC.
Motivation for being part of the EFC It is such a great honour to be able to work with world-class performers, orchestras and conductors. We may be an amateur Chorus, but we always work to professional standards.
What do you find especially fulfilling about being part of the EFC? It's a lot of hard work throughout the year, but when we reach that part of the year where we practise with the orchestra and the soloists, everything clicks into place. All of our hard work throughout the year has paid off – it is the best feeling. I also really enjoy working with Christopher Bell. I love his attention to detail. ■

Name Brendan Glen
Year joined 2011
Most memorable concert
Bernstein's *Kaddish*
Symphony in 2014.
**Motivation for being
part of the EFC** The
works I have taken part
in have provided me with
experiences and challenges
that I would have otherwise
not received.
**What do you find
especially fulfilling about
being part of the EFC?**
What's most rewarding
is when the hard work
put into a challenging
piece pays off. One of the
best things about being
in the EFC is getting to
perform alongside so many
exceptional orchestras and
musicians from all over the
world. With the EFC, I have
taken part in some rather
special performances of
works that I would not have
had the chance to perform,
and the temptation of more
excellent concerts is why
I want to continue. ∎

Name Janet McKenzie
Year joined 1990
Most memorable concert
The Mozart Requiem with
Leningrad Philharmonic
and Yuri Temirkanov in
1991. We were rehearsing
when news of the attempted
coup in Moscow came
through. It was a concert
charged with emotion.
**Motivation for being part
of the EFC** I love singing,
and the EFC's standard
of musicianship is what
motivates me.
**What do you find
especially fulfilling about
being part of the EFC?**
The music; the opportunity
to sing with some of the
best orchestras and best
conductors around; the
achievement of pulling
off some challenging
pieces; the amazing sense
of being part of a team; the
support and friendship
I enjoy; and the inspiring
leadership we have had
from our Chorus Masters
over the years. ∎

Name John McLeod
Year joined 2004
Most memorable concert
Weill's *The Rise and Fall
of the City of Mahagonny*
with HK Gruber in 2008
was memorable (in a mad
way), but I would always
go back to Mahler's Eighth
Symphony (2010).
**Motivation for being
part of the EFC** To sing
in concerts performed
to the highest possible
standard, experiencing
pieces that most ensembles
would not get the chance
to sing, because of the
forces required or the sheer
musical difficulty.
**What do you find
especially fulfilling about
being part of the EFC?**
Sometimes, conductors
who have not worked with
us before are so obviously
delighted with the sound
they hear at their first
rehearsal. The flip side of
that is that when they come
back, they will expect even
better things from us! ∎

Name María Liendo Zaccara
Year joined 2014
**Most memorable
concert** Beethoven's
Ninth Symphony with the
BBC Scottish Symphony
Orchestra for conductor
Donald Runnicles' 60th
birthday – it was brilliant!
**What do you find
especially fulfilling about
being part of the EFC?**
We get the opportunity to
perform great repertoire,
which varies every year
for each Festival, so we
are able to explore many
different composers, styles,
languages and so on. The
quality of the orchestras
and conductors we get to
work with would also be
very difficult to match in
any other chorus of this
type, in Scotland or in the
rest of the UK. Although
I have only been part of the
EFC for a short time, I am
already excited thinking
what we might sing in
future years. I feel very
lucky to be part of it. ∎

Cherished objects, cuttings and memories from
the Edinburgh Festival Chorus' 50-year history

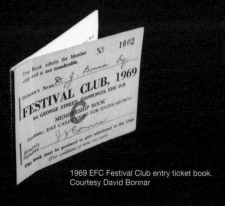

1969 EFC Festival Club entry ticket book.
Courtesy David Bonnar

Programme from what was the Scottish Festival Chorus' inaugural
1965 Festival performance, with glowing press coverage

Early EFC car sticker

Intricate arrangements: a Scottish Festival
Chorus rehearsal and performance
schedule from 1965

The all-important acceptance letter: former EFC
singer David Bonnar's 1968 invitation from
Arthur Oldham to join the EFC

Programme and leaflet for the EFC's 1984 concert
in Munich, celebrating the 30th anniversary of the
twinning of Munich and Edinburgh

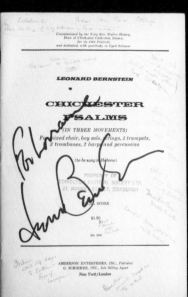

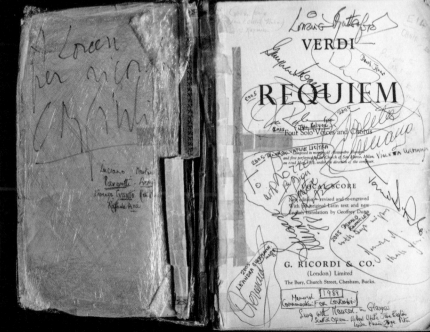

A history of autographs: EFC member Lorraine Veitch Rutherford's scores, signed by (among many others) Leonard Bernstein, Violetta Urmana, Yuri Temirkanov, Alexander Lazarev, Valery Gergiev, Daniil Trifonov, Luciano Pavarotti and Donald Runnicles

The EFC's newsletter, *Vox*, in its first issue from 1997

Sir Charles Mackerras wishes the EFC singers well in their performances of Haydn's *Creation* and Mendelssohn's *Elijah*, 1996

Leaflet and touring instructions (complete with hand-drawn map) from the EFC's Israel performances of Handel's *Israel in Egypt* in 1981–2

Leaflet and programme for the EFC's 1990 performances in the Basilique de Saint-Denis, Paris

Rueful souvenir of the EFC's most notoriously challenging work, Schoenberg's opera *Moses and Aaron*, from 1992

Two of the EFC's many
commercial recordings:
Mozart's *Così fan tutte* (1993)
and Mendelssohn's *Elijah* (1996)

All you need to know:
EFC handbooks from 2009 to 2015

The EFC's 40th anniversary celebration publication,
from 2005

The Zimmermann project: programme,
leaflet and CD cover from the 1995
performances and recording of the
Requiem for a Young Poet

Impromptu sketching: artist Ian Stuart
Campbell's drawing of the EFC in concert,
inside a 2014 EIF concert programme

Diary of a newbie

The 2014 Festival was tenor Ian Phillips' first as a member of the Edinburgh Festival Chorus. He kept a diary of his thoughts on the excitement of rehearsals, performances – and doing the hokey-cokey

31 JULY 2014

Finding a venue to accommodate 130 singers to rehearse during the Edinburgh festivals season is no mean feat. Every potential space seems to have been earmarked for some kind of performance. The Edinburgh Academy Junior School Assembly Hall turns out to be ideal – even though it is not great for bus routes. I have a few close calls trying to drive around Edinburgh and being there on time.

4 AUGUST 2014

For me, suddenly performing for a new conductor (instead of the Chorus Master) is initially quite unsettling. You are familiar with the tempo, nuances, volume, pronunciation and so on that you've rehearsed – and they will, inevitably, do things differently. High-level concentration is required. I wonder if they ever change their planned approach when they hear what we actually sound like.

Our conductor for the Opening Concert is Oliver Knussen, who helps set the scene for what turns out to be a regular sequence of events: run-through with conductor and piano; rehearsals with orchestra; and then the concert. Through each stage you become more confident about what will be just a single performance. I want to ensure that I do what I can to reflect the work we've put in, and to ensure that I'll be asked back for a second year! You cannot be tentative, you cannot be nearly on the right note, and you cannot just follow those around you. You need to be on the button.

Rehearsal breaks are a chance to meet fellow EFC members. Even after a year, you see people in the tea queue who you've never seen before. Or people asking who you are, even though you've said hello before. And don't even try to remember names!

8 AUGUST 2014

The Opening Concert

I find the Usher Hall rehearsals with orchestra just as enjoyable as the performance itself. The space encourages you to deliver and adds further quality to the overall sound. The final rehearsal might have you singing at performance standard – although, for some pieces, it's recommended that you hold a little something back for the main event. For Scriabin's *Prometheus – The Poem of Fire*, it's certainly volume we go for. Our second piece, Debussy's *Le martyre de Saint Sébastien*, is more poetic and allows us to demonstrate some light and shade.

At the concert there is the sense that the EFC is suddenly on maximum concentration, that all the work seems to come into focus, so that we sound at our peak. You become immersed in the music – or at least I do. To be able to sing

Diligent EFC rehearsals in 2014

Photos Stuart Armitt; Clark James

among wonderful musicians, and to create sounds that cause emotion in both ourselves and the audience, really is a privilege.

14 AUGUST 2014
Britten's *War Requiem*

There's usually a short break between the final afternoon rehearsal and the performance. This two-hour slot can be problematic. Eating and/or drinking is something to consider carefully – to ensure you don't have anything heavy on the stomach that will affect your singing. On this occasion I settle on chilli con carne and tonic water. Look around the various eating establishments near the Usher Hall on the afternoon of a concert day and you can always find someone eating a meal in their dinner jacket.

During the break I also have a chat with our conductor, Sir Andrew Davis, to explain this is all new to me and that I'm enjoying it very much. I'm not sure protocol allows such lowly members of the EFC to approach conductors, but it doesn't seem to bother him.

My second concert is the first that my family and friends are able to attend. Although there have been reviews of the first concert, it really is what your own loved ones think that matters. Looking out to the audience you try to

Conductor Sir Andrew Davis in rehearsal, 2014

Photo Clark James

identify them. You sometimes catch them smiling or even waving at you. Of course we sit still and don't even raise an eyebrow in acknowledgement. Thankfully, they love the concert. It's at this time you suddenly think: what do we actually sound like? You never get the chance to experience what the audience does.

I thought this concert was going to be the emotional highlight of the year. With its links with the Festival theme of war and conflict, Britten's *War Requiem* demands immersion and conviction. It's strange to suggest that such a sad and difficult piece is also one that brings enjoyment – but it does.

Advice to new chorus members: if a concert is on a Thursday night and you plan on going for a wee refreshment afterwards, it's highly recommended that you take a day's holiday on the Friday. The Traverse bar runs out of wine glasses tonight.

22 AUGUST 2014
Bernstein's *Kaddish* Symphony

The rehearsal routine is slightly adjusted to accommodate a trip to Glasgow's Royal Concert Hall for rehearsal. Conductor John Axelrod introduces me (and most of the EFC) to some new rehearsal techniques – with unexpected levels of participation and movement. Although most of what happens in rehearsal stays in rehearsal, I think admitting that we sing the hokey-cokey gives some idea of the first meeting with the conductor. I'm not sure there's full participation on the in-out-in-out-shake-it-all-about.

Singing in Hebrew is new to me. Even being Scottish and used to rolling Rs and throaty CH doesn't prepare me for getting the pronunciation on this one sorted. Never before have I discussed diphthongs so much.

For me, this concert is a highlight. The emotional text, narrated with such depth and realism by Samuel Pisar, has the audience on its feet in appreciation. A few, myself included, have a tear in their eye.

30 AUGUST 2014
The Closing Concert

I'm transfixed by the percussion section. They normally spread out in front of the Chorus on stage, strategically placing tubular bells, tam-tam and bass drum so that we can't see the conductor.

This concert involves a great deal of both standard and exotic percussion – including hubcaps and water-filled tubs from IKEA. The effect is quite startling. Until, that is, a leak begins to spring from a tub. I think the leak begins when a rearrangement of the percussion is called for, so that we can see the conductor.

All this percussion is there for the performance of outgoing Festival Director Sir Jonathan Mills' *Sandakan Threnody*. This is a piece that requires counting. And concentration. And some more counting.

The final notes of our final concert are those of Janáček's *Glagolitic Mass*. They certainly blow away the cobwebs – if any remained.

It is the end of the season of performances, and also the end of my first year in the EFC. Singing in the Chorus has been a commitment of time and effort, but it's been worth it. There are some things I've enjoyed more than others, but I think every piece has provided us with musical challenges, and with some less comfortable moments. But that's the fun, and the real sign of doing something well. I've just managed to sneak in to what have been the EFC's first 50 years, and I'm very glad I have. ■

The 'silent backbone'

Chorus Manager Helen MacLeod talks to Peter Somerford about the challenges and rewards of running the EFC, from the stresses of arranging auditions to coach breakdowns on the M8

Organising auditions and language coaches, booking venues and transport, arranging music hire and purchase, and communicating with the Chorus Master and EFC members are, quite literally, all in a day's work for Helen MacLeod. As Chorus Manager of the Edinburgh Festival Chorus, she has an important and hugely varied role. In addition, she provides administrative support to the Festival's Artistic Planning department – a second role that she estimates takes up a third of her time.

MacLeod arrived in July 2008, and had always wanted to work in music. 'I did a geography degree but was heavily involved in music at university,' she says. 'I was orchestra manager for one of the student orchestras, and saw myself doing something similar after university.' She had previously studied part-time for a research-based Master's in music – her dissertation subject was the Edinburgh International Festival.

MacLeod played flute and piano to a high standard but is not a singer. 'I'm very much the silent backbone,' she quips, adding: 'Working with the

> *'There have been times when coaches have broken down, or been stuck in jams on the M8, but everything's always come together'*

EFC has opened up a huge range of repertoire that I had never engaged with before.' Aside from discovering great choral music, MacLeod says one of the best aspects of her job has been getting to know the EFC members. 'They're a fantastic bunch of people,' she says. 'I want to help make their involvement in the EFC as fulfilling as possible.' She stays in close contact with the members once the rehearsal season begins in mid-October, dealing with attendance issues and keeping the EFC up to speed with any changes to rehearsal schedules. 'Making sure everyone is in the right place at the right time is an essential part of the job,' she says. 'I'm also conscious that

people have busy lives away from the EFC, so there is something of a balance between maintaining the artistic integrity and ambition of the EFC and knowing that the members have all kinds of other commitments. But the dedication they show to the EFC is outstanding.'

As the first point of contact for prospective members, MacLeod arranges auditions for the EFC, which mostly take place in late September and early October. 'We usually have between 30 and 60 people auditioning in any one season,' she explains, 'but that includes some who might audition in November or December. Even if they've missed too many rehearsals of one work, they can still sing in other works.' Not everyone gets in, of course, and it usually falls to MacLeod to deliver the news of their success or failure. 'Sometimes the Chorus Master might tell them at the end of the audition,' she says, 'but generally I let them know by letter whether it's a yes or a no.'

As well as communicating with the full-time members, MacLeod also handles arrangements for 'augmenters' – singers who aren't able to commit to permanent membership but are invited to sing certain works that need extra voices. Dealing with additional personnel adds an extra layer to MacLeod's responsibilities, but that doesn't seem to faze her: 'It's great that we can give more singers the opportunity to take part, and it just means I get to deal with more and more people who are involved in the performance.'

MacLeod's workload has also increased with the addition of concerts outside the Festival. These have included two visits to the BBC Proms, in 2010 and 2011, as well as regular concerts with the BBC Scottish Symphony Orchestra during its season. 'The travel and accommodation for a Proms appearance can be difficult to organise,' MacLeod admits, 'but I see how a concert away like that brings

the EFC closer together. It's a great bonding experience.' The EFC has yet to perform overseas during her tenure, but MacLeod gives the impression that she would relish the logistical challenges. 'Getting everyone to the airport at the same time would be fun, for sure,' she says.

When pressed for tales of behind-the-scenes logistical dramas, MacLeod can't recall any drastic emergencies. 'There have been times when coaches have broken down, or been stuck in jams on the M8,' she says, 'but everything's always come together. I guess I take those moments for granted: you just have to get on with the job and ensure everything turns out right.'

Looking back to her early days in the position, MacLeod says she inherited some work practices from

Former EFC Administrators
Alastair Dewar and Margery Ramsay

Margery Ramsay, her long-serving predecessor. Ramsay became the Chorus Administrator in 1992, taking over from Alastair Dewar, a former BBC Radio Scotland sports broadcaster who had been the Administrator since 1975. Ramsay, like MacLeod, performed a dual role: in her case, she also worked as Assistant to the Associate Festival Director. 'There was so much information to take on board when I started,' says MacLeod, 'so it was good to see how things were done. Christopher Bell had only joined a year before as Chorus Master and was already making changes, so to some extent I was led by the changes he was making. But I was also given support to do things in the way that I found worked best. Every Festival is different, so it's become natural to adapt the way I do certain parts of the job.'

Just like the EFC members, MacLeod can quickly reel off her personal musical highlights from her time in the post – among them the 2014 performance of Britten's *War Requiem*, and the 'overwhelming experience' of Mahler's Symphony No 2 in 2011. Yet what she cherishes even more than the music is seeing the elation and excitement on the faces of the EFC after a triumphant performance. 'The greatest joy for me is when I hear the audience roar, when the Chorus stand to take their bow and then come off stage happy at the end of a performance. That's when I know they've achieved something incredible.' ■

Crucial contributions:
Chorus Manager Helen MacLeod

Stuart Armitt

A life with the Chorus

Not only has Donald Runnicles directed the Edinburgh Festival Chorus in more concerts than any other conductor, but he also sang – as a ten-year-old chorister – in the Chorus' inaugural performance. He reveals to Ken Walton the enormous impact the EFC has had on his career

Ken Friedman

The ladies of the Edinburgh Festival Chorus have a habit of reminding Donald Runnicles that, as a ten-year-old, he was there with them at the birth of the Chorus he now loves to conduct. 'Whenever I come back, they proudly produce a photograph of me singing in the boys' choir for Mahler Eight, standing behind the horn section of the then Scottish National Orchestra,' says the maestro who, half a century on, is now one of the world's most respected opera and large-scale symphonic conductors.

The year was 1965, and Runnicles – then a pupil at George Watson's College – had been drafted in, along with other Edinburgh schoolboys, for the inaugural Festival concert by the newly formed Scottish Festival Chorus. What does he recall of the event? How his future calling? With hindsight, he says, it set him on several journeys. 'In some way with the music of Mahler; in some way as a conductor; and in my long association with the Edinburgh Festival Chorus.'

So what does he actually recall from that historic evening on 22 August 1965, the opening concert of that year's Festival? What was it like to be part of this newly assembled Chorus? To be trained by Arthur Oldham, the man charged with bringing this massive new army of singers together for the first time? And ultimately to perform under the baton of Alexander Gibson, then at his prime as Artistic Director of the SNO?

'I remember, in the best sense, the fierce discipline demanded by Arthur Oldham, his uncompromising approach to find – as my father would have said in front of his own Morningside church choir – a unanimity of tone. And I remember the boys being given a variety of exercises to get us warmed up – we had to sing "Popocatepetl" over three or four octaves, and that's stuck with me forever.'

Oldham demanded nothing less than perfection, Runnicles adds. 'He was a force of nature, inimitable, unique, and just glowed with this ardent advocacy. Very few people could have got away with his promiscuous swearing. He settled for nothing less than complete homogeneity of sound and rhythm, and he couldn't stand it when people sang flat. I didn't encounter that kind of disciplined approach until years later when I worked with the Atlanta Symphony Orchestra Chorus, where the legacy of the legendary Robert Shaw was still alive and well. I immediately recognised a similarity in approach between singing with Arthur Oldham in the 1960s and then, so many years later, to be at the helm of this equally great force in Atlanta.'

If, in 1965, Oldham left the young Runnicles open-mouthed in awe and admiration, so did Gibson. 'He came later in the rehearsal process. I just remember this charismatic conductor with flapping tails. The whole experience was one of wonder to me, that so many people could come together and could be of one purpose. On so many levels for me that night – including the chance to perform on the same stage as the likes of Janet Baker and Heather Harper – seeds were sown.'

One of these seeds was an early baptism into the world of Mahler, whose symphonies were undergoing a significant renaissance in the 1960s, thanks largely to the pioneering work of Leonard Bernstein. But it was the Eighth in particular that was to remain a constant within that special relationship Runnicles has continued to enjoy with the EFC 'from the other side of the horn section'.

For it was again that very Symphony that Runnicles found himself in charge of at his conducting debut with the EFC in 1994. He had made his actual Edinburgh International Festival debut the previous year, but when EIF Director Brian McMaster approached him about coming back for Mahler's Eighth, the decision, he says, was a no-brainer.

'It just seemed so wonderfully poetic; so meaningful, having been part of the inaugural concert all those years before, and now there at the front leading this phenomenal performance of the same work. And who was the Chorus Master? It was Arthur Oldham, and we reminisced a great deal about the EFC and his methods. It seemed I'd come full circle.'

That was also with the SNO – by that stage the Royal Scottish National Orchestra. But fast forward to 2001, ➡

Donald Runnicles with the EFC and BBC Scottish Symphony Orchestra at the opening concert of the 2005 Festival

Peter Sandground

when the EFC played a major role in an opening-night performance of Berlioz's epic opera *The Trojans* that was to mark the start of Runnicles' now legendary relationship with the BBC Scottish Symphony Orchestra. 'When I reflect on it, I realise the EFC has been there at so many pivotal moments in my career. But for them to have been part of my first concert with the BBC SSO means so much to me.'

Barely a Festival has since passed when Runnicles, the BBC SSO and EFC have not been a notable presence. He rattles off the highlights: Wagner's opera *Lohengrin*, Britten's *War Requiem*, Berlioz and Verdi Requiems, and of course, yet another Mahler Eighth Symphony in 2010, which was the resounding climax to that year's Festival. Significantly, too, he chose the EFC to feature in the concert celebrating his own 60th birthday, with the BBC SSO in November 2014, a performance of yet an other great musical Everest, Beethoven's Ninth Symphony.

Fifty years on from his boyhood initiation, and now a veteran of the international concert circuit and opera world – including a 17-year tenure as Music Director of San Francisco Opera, and his current Directorship of Berlin's Deutsche Oper – Runnicles is well qualified to appraise the EFC in an international context.

'I think it's a very fine Chorus,' he says. 'The man who started it, Arthur Oldham, is owed a great debt of gratitude, and his successors have continued that great tradition. But I'll be frank. I think the past few years under Christopher Bell have been really important in the EFC's development. I think he's brought them into a new league where they can fearlessly tackle repertoire that, a few years ago, might have been more challenging. They are now, without doubt, one of the greatest choruses in the world.' ∎

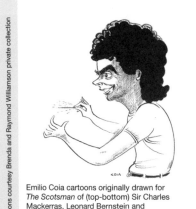

Cartoons courtesy Brenda and Raymond Williamson private collection

Emilio Coia cartoons originally drawn for *The Scotsman* of (top-bottom) Sir Charles Mackerras, Leonard Bernstein and Sir Simon Rattle

The year is 1980. It's the closing night of the Edinburgh International Festival. A speeding police car hurtles through the West End city streets, siren blaring. It careers to a halt outside the Usher Hall. Out rushes virtuoso organist Gillian Weir.

As she hurries inside to join conductor Claudio Abbado, the London Symphony Orchestra and Edinburgh Festival Chorus on stage for the final curtain call, Weir recalls hearing the words 'one minute 20 seconds' – the time it took to get there – from Festival Director John Drummond, whose crazy idea it was to have the organ part of Berlioz's Te Deum played a mile away in St Mary's Episcopal Cathedral and beamed live to the Usher Hall as an integral part of the performance.

Such crazy moments can make being part of the EFC a very different experience from other choral singing. But more importantly it's also about working with the world's greatest conductors, feeding off their inevitable charisma and musical influence – even if the context, as in this case, can be unconventional.

A frequent EFC conductor: Claudio Abbado

Living legends

Many of the world's pre-eminent conductors have directed the EFC during its 50-year history. Ken Walton looks back on some of the most illustrious figures

Abbado, whose golden orchestral and operatic pedigree encompassed musical directorships of La Scala and the Vienna State Opera, the Berlin Philharmonic and his own Gustav Mahler Youth Orchestra, returned to conduct the EFC with the LSO in 1982, in a more conventional performance of Verdi's Requiem, the live (now DVD) recording of which still ranks among the finest available on the archive market.

Inevitably, the list of conductors associated with landmark EFC performances reads like a who's who of late 20th-century conducting greats. But ask long-standing EFC members who

Carlo Maria Giulini: a magisterial *War Requiem* in 1968

Alex 'Tug' Wilson

made the biggest impact and an interesting selection appears.

Sir Georg Solti is remembered for his 1982 Beethoven *Missa solemnis* with great affection, particularly as he insisted on having the EFC repeat the performance at the BBC Proms in London two days later. Tenor Ken Ballantine, with 33 Festivals behind him, recalls how Solti's ability to get the best out of the EFC was reciprocated by kindness on their part. 'He had the flu in Edinburgh and we gave him some malt whisky,' Ballantine explains. 'Two days later in London, Solti announced that he was feeling much better, but that "the whisky bottle was much worse".'

Sir Simon Rattle is another strong memory for Ballantine. 'He was very good at explaining things, painting pictures through his marvellous similes'. As for Colin Davis, his 'infectious sense of humour' struck a lingering chord.

But the name that rolls most frequently off the tongues of EFC singers is Sir Charles Mackerras. 'He was a real singer's conductor who understood what made us tick,' says Ballantine, remembering particularly the pungent Beethoven Ninth Symphony with the Philharmonia Orchestra that concluded Mackerras' complete

Beethoven symphony series in 2006. 'He was like a favourite uncle,' adds EFC alto Rosamund Davidson.

There are many who came as living legends – among them Daniel Barenboim, Riccardo Muti, Yuri Temirkanov, David Robertson, Riccardo Chailly, Valery Gergiev, Sir Andrew Davis, Mariss Jansons and, of course, Sir Alexander Gibson – whose magical connection with the EFC and Festival were simply golden moments in EIF history. As was that of the magisterial Carlo Maria Giulini, whose 1968 performance of Britten's *War Requiem*, with Britten himself present, was the first ever performance to feature the originally intended soloists – soprano Galina Vishnevskaya had been unable to sing in the 1962 premiere at Coventry Cathedral alongside Peter Pears and Dietrich Fischer-Dieskau.

Five years later, Leonard Bernstein's brilliant 1973 Festival performance of Mahler's 'Resurrection' Symphony, better known perhaps from its subsequent televised recording in Ely Cathedral, was a stunning example of Bernstein at the height of his Mahler crusade.

Life in the Edinburgh Festival Chorus is inextricably bound up with conducting legends. ∎

Rehearsals, and relaxing pre- and post-concerts: EFC singers

Orchestras and ensembles

Instrumental groups with which the EFC has performed, plus numbers of performances

- 6 Alexander von Schlippenbach Jazz Combo
- 1 Australian Youth Orchestra
- 3 Bamberg Symphony Orchestra
- 1 Bavarian Radio Symphony Orchestra
- 1 BBC Philharmonic Orchestra
- 1 BBC Scottish Symphony Orchestra
- 44 BBC Symphony Orchestra
- 2 Berlin Philharmonic Orchestra
- 3 Berlin Symphony Orchestra
- 1 Boston Symphony Orchestra
- 2 Budapest Festival Orchestra
- 1 City of Birmingham Symphony Orchestra
- 1 City of London Sinfonia
- 1 Cleveland Orchestra
- 2 Czech Philharmonic Orchestra
- 1 Equale Brass
- 2 European Union Youth Orchestra
- 2 Finnish Radio Symphony Orchestra
- 2 Graunke Symphony Orchestra
- 6 Gustav Mahler Jugendorchester
- 1 Hallé Orchestra
- 5 Houston Symphony Orchestra
- 5 Jerusalem Symphony Orchestra
- 3 Junge Deutsche Philharmonie
- 19 Leningrad Philharmonic Orchestra
- 35 London Philharmonic Orchestra
- 2 London Symphony Orchestra
- 1 Los Angeles Philharmonic Orchestra
- 4 Moscow Radio Orchestra
- 10 National Orchestra of Spain
- 2 New Philharmonia Orchestra
- 6 Nouvel Orchestre Philharmonique
- 4 Orchestre de Paris
- 2 Orchestra of Scottish Opera
- 2 Orchestra of the Age of Enlightenment
- 2 Orchestra of the Bolshoi Theatre
- 2 Orchestra of the Maggio Musicale
- 4 Orchestre de l'Opéra de Lyon
- 3 Orchestre National de France
- 1 Oslo Philharmonic Orchestra
- 12 Philharmonia Orchestra
- 3 Pittsburgh Symphony Orchestra
- 1 Prague Symphony Orchestra
- 2 Radio Filharmonisch Orkest Holland
- 1 Rotterdam Philharmonic Orchestra
- 21 Royal Concertgebouw Orchestra
- 80 Royal Philharmonic Orchestra
- 2 Russian National Orchestra
- 6 Scottish Chamber Orchestra
- 2 Royal Scottish National Orchestra
- 1 Swedish Radio Symphony Orchestra
- 1 SWF Symphony Orchestra, Baden-Baden
- 2 Sydney Symphony Orchestra
- 1 Tchaikovsky Symphony Orchestra of Moscow Radio
- 2 The Hanover Band
- 1 The Wallace Collection
- Tonhalle Orchestra Zurich
- Toronto Symphony Orchestra
- Vienna Philharmonic Orchestra
- 1 World War 1 Commemoration / Military Bands

Languages

Numbers of performances in the EFC's broad range of languages

- 8 Czech
- 46 English
- 1 Finnish
- 35 French
- 100 German
- 4 Hebrew
- 8 Italian
- 101 Latin
- 16 Wordless
- 1 Polish
- 17 Russian
- 5 Spanish

Choirs and choruses

Vocal groups that have sung with the EFC, plus numbers of performances

- 1 Alexander Gibson Opera School
- 1 Arnold Schoenberg Choir
- 1 BBC Singers
- 6 Bratislava City Chorus
- 1 Brighton Festival Chorus
- 1 Capella Nova
- 1 Cleveland Orchestra Chorus
- 3 John Currie Singers
- 6 Kölner Rundfunkchor
- 2 National Youth Choir of Scotland
- 2 National Youth Choir of Scotland, National Boys Choir
- 3 National Youth Choir of Scotland, National Girls Choir
- 1 Philharmonia Chorus
- 1 Prague Philharmonic Choir
- 3 Royal Scottish Academy of Music and Drama Choristers
- 11 Royal Scottish National Orchestra Junior Chorus
- 4 Scottish National Orchestra Chorus
- 6 Slovakian Philharmonic Chorus, Bratislava
- 1 Stewart's Melville School Choir
- 6 Südfunkchor, Stuttgart

Conductors

The illustrious figures who have conducted the EFC, plus numbers of performances

- 16 Claudio Abbado
- 4 Richard Armstrong
- 1 John Axelrod
- 1 Daniel Barenboim
- 1 Michael Bawtree
- 2 Jiří Bělohlávek
- 1 Maurizio Benini
- 1 Leonard Bernstein
- 2 Gary Bertini
- 1 Sir Adrian Boult
- 1 Benjamin Britten
- 5 Riccardo Chailly
- 2 William Christie
- 5 Myung-Whun Chung
- 1 Francesco Corti
- 5 John Currie
- 5 Paul Daniel
- 1 John Dankworth
- 1 Sir Andrew Davis
- 2 Colin Davis
- 1 Reinbert de Leeuw
- 3 Stéphane Denève
- 2 Charles Dutoit
- 2 Sir Mark Elder
- 4 John Eliot Gardiner
- 2 Vladimir Fedoseyev
- 6 Iván Fischer
- 2 Claus Peter Flor
- Rafael Frühbeck de Burgos
- Edward Gardner
- Valery Gergiev
- Sir Alexander Gibson
- 15 Michael Gielen
- Carlo Maria Giulini
- Hans Graf
- HK Gruber
- 1 Leopold Hager
- Emmanuelle Haïm
- Bernard Haitink
- Günther Herbig
- Richard Hickox
- 2 Marek Janowski
- 3 Mariss Jansons
- Neeme Järvi
- 1 David Jones
- 2 Vladimir Jurowski
- 2 István Kertész
- 1 Oliver Knussen
- 1 Rafael Kubelik
- 1 Alexander Lazarev
- 2 Jesús López-Cobos
- 1 James Loughran
- 1 Witold Lutosławski
- 17 Sir Charles Mackerras
- 1 James MacMillan
- 1 Susanna Mälkki
- 1 Cristian Mandeal
- 1 Andrew Manze
- 1 John Mauceri
- 1 Lorin Maazel
- 1 Yehudi Menuhin
- 6 Riccardo Muti
- 1 John Nelson
- 2 Roger Norrington
- 3 Gianandrea Noseda
- 5 Jonathan Nott
- 1 Arthur Oldham
- 6 Peter Oundjian
- 5 Seiji Ozawa
- 1 Mikhail Pletnev
- 3 Andre Previn
- 3 Sir Simon Rattle
- 1 John Pritchard
- 1 Carlo Rizzi
- 4 David Robertson
- 26 Mstislav Rostropovich
- 2 Gennady Rozhdestvensky
- 1 Donald Runnicles
- 2 Esa-Pekka Salonen
- 4 Kwamé Ryan
- Jukka-Pekka Saraste
- 1 Stanisław Skrowaczewski
- 3 Yuri Simonov
- 2 Sir Georg Solti
- 4 Giuseppe Sinopoli
- Robert Spano
- Joseph Swensen
- Yan Tortelier
- Robin Ticciati
- Michael Tilson Thomas
- Bramwell Tovey
- Willem van Otterloo
- Ilan Volkov
- Christoph von Dohnányi
- Oliver von Dohnányi
- Herbert von Karajan
- Hans Vonk
- Garry Walker
- Walter Weller
- Mark Wigglesworth
- David Zinman

Composers and works

Composers and repertoire that the EFC has performed, plus numbers of performances

Brahms
- 11 Ein deutsches Requiem
- 1 Schicksalslied
- 1 Liebeslieder Waltzes
- 1 Gesang der Parzen
- 1 Four Songs

Weber
- 6 Oberon
- 1 Euryanthe

Beethoven
- 1 Mass in C
- 14 Symphony No 9
- 1 Leonora
- 1 Fidelio
- 2 Christ on the Mount of Olives
- 5 Choral Fantasia
- 7 Missa solemnis

Britten
- 2 Alto Rhapsody
- 5 War Requiem
- 1 Voices for Today
- 1 The Building of the House
- 3 Spring Symphony
- 2 National Anthem
- 2 Cantata academica

Debussy
- 5 Nocturnes
- 1 Le martyre de Saint Sébastien

Mozart
- 5 Requiem
- 1 Mass in C minor
- 1 Mass in C
- 1 Così fan tutte
- 1 Laudate Dominum
- 1 Kyrie in D minor
- 1 Idomeneo

Dvořák
- 3 Requiem
- 1 Te Deum
- 1 Stabat Mater
- 1 Saint Ludmila

Mahler
- 15 Symphony No 2 'Resurrection'
- 1 Das klagende Lied
- 5 Symphony No 8
- 6 Symphony No 3

Ravel
- 9 Daphnis et Chloé

Handel
- 3 Israel in Egypt
- 1 Saul
- 1 Judas Maccabaeus
- 1 Jephtha

Berlioz
- 6 The Damnation of Faust
- 1 The Trojans at Carthage
- 1 The Siege of Troy
- 2 La Marseillaise
- 5 Grande messe des morts
- 3 Roméo et Juliette
- 4 Te Deum

Bruckner
- 3 Locus Iste/Ave Maria
- 1 Mass in F minor
- 1 Mass in E minor
- 3 Te Deum

Janáček
- 5 Glagolitic Mass
- 1 Amarus

Prokofiev
- 6 Alexander Nevsky
- 1 War and Peace Suite
- 1 Seven, They Are Seven

Rossini
- 4 Stabat Mater
- 1 Petite messe solennelle
- 1 La donna del lago

Verdi
- 12 Requiem
- 1 Stabat Mater
- 1 Oberto, conte di San Bonifacio
- 1 Giovanna d'Arco
- 2 Te Deum
- 2 Macbeth
- 3 Four Sacred Pieces

Stravinsky
- 3 Oedipus rex
- 2 Le roi des étoiles
- 3 Symphony of Psalms

Wagner
- 1 Die Meistersinger von Nürnberg
- 1 Tristan und Isolde
- 1 Götterdämmerung A
- 1 Siegfried Act 2
- 1 Lohengrin
- 1 Lohengin Act 2

6 Requiem for
a Young Poet

Zimmermann

2 Gurrelieder

Schoenberg

1 Moses
and Aaron

1 A Survivor
from Warsaw

1 Requiem

1 Requiem No 2

Cherubini

5 Requiem

Fauré

1 Mass in E flat

1 Three
Songs

1 Mass No 5

1 Mass No 6

Schubert

2 A Mass of Life

Delius

3 Das Paradies und die Peri

Schumann

1 Scenes from
Goethe's Faust

1 Moscow Cantata

1 Manfred

2 Liturgy of St John Chrysostom

Tchaikovsky

1 1812 Overture

1 Jeanne d'Arc au bûcher

1 Le roi David

Honegger

5 A Child of Our Time

Tippett

2 A Sea Symphony

2 Dona nobis
pacem

Vaughan Williams

2 Faust Symphony

Liszt

5 Belshazzar's Feast

Walton

2 Harmonium

1 El niño

Adams

1 In Praise of the Virgin

1 Psalms in
Time of War

Oldham

1 Kaddish
Symphony
No 3

2 Chichester Psalms

Bernstein

1 Candide

2 St Matthew Passion

1 Magnificat

Bach

2 Carmina Burana

Orff

2 Atlántida

Falla

2 La vida breve

3 The Dream
of Gerontius

Elgar

2 Blest Pair of Sirens

Parry

4 The Creation

Poulenc

1 Stabat Mater

Haydn

1 Dialogues des
Carmélites

1 Folksongs

1 Symphony No 1

1 Prometheus,
The Poem of Fire

Scriabin

3 The Planets

1 Turn Back, O Man

Holst

1 Four Hungarian
Folksongs

1 The Miraculous
Mandarin

Bartók

2 Te Deum

Wilson

- **Busoni**
  1 Piano Concerto
- **Enescu**
  1 Oedipe
- **Grainger**
  1 Songs for soloists and chorus
- **Kodály**
  1 Psalmus hungaricus
- **Lesueur**
  1 Ossian's Dream
- **Lloyd Webber**
  1 Joseph and the Amazing
  Technicolor Dreamcoat (excerpts)
- **Lutosławski**
  1 Poèmes d'Henri Michaux
- **MacMillan**
  1 Quickening
- **Martinů**
  1 The Greek Passion
- **Massenet**
  1 Thaïs
- **Matthews**
  1 Pluto
- **Méhul**
  1 Uthal
- **Mendelssohn**
  1 Elijah
- **Messiaen**
  1 Saint François d'Assise
- **Mills**
  1 Sandakan Threnody
- **Oliver**
  1 Namings
- **Petrassi**
  1 Magnificat
- **Puccini**
  1 La fanciulla del West
- **Rachmaninov**
  1 The Bells
- **Seter**
  1 Jerusalem, Symphony for mixed choir
- **Sibelius**
  1 Kullervo
- **Smetana**
  1 Libuše
- **Strauss**
  1 Elektra
- **Szymanowski**
  1 Symphony No 3 'Song of the Night'
- **Tallis**
  1 Spem in alium
- **Weill**
  1 The Rise and Fall of
  the City of Mahagonny
- **Wolf**
  1 Der Feuerreiter
- **Vivaldi**
  1 Gloria

Fifty years of exceptional performances

Complete listings of a half-century of concerts from the Edinburgh Festival Chorus

All concerts in Edinburgh's Usher Hall unless otherwise stated

1965

Festival Director:
George, Earl of Harewood
(1961–1965)
Chorus Master:
Arthur Oldham (1965–1977)

22 AUGUST 1965
Mahler: Symphony No 8
(Scottish premiere)
Heather Harper (soprano)
Gwynneth Jones (soprano)
Gwenyth Annear (soprano)
Janet Baker (mezzo soprano)
Norma Procter (contralto)
Vilem Pribyl (tenor)
Vladimir Ruzdjak (baritone)
Donald McIntyre (bass)
Scottish Festival Chorus
  (original name of EFC)
Scottish National Orchestra/
  Alexander Gibson

1966

Festival Director:
Peter Diamand (1966–1978)

21 AUGUST 1966
Britten: Cantata academica
Tippett: A Child of Our Time
Elizabeth Vaughan (soprano)
Janet Baker (mezzo soprano)
Richard Lewis (tenor)
Forbes Robinson (bass)
Scottish Festival Chorus
Scottish National Orchestra/
  Alexander Gibson

24 AUGUST 1966
Prokofiev:
  Seven, They Are Seven
Vilem Pribyl (tenor)
Scottish Festival Chorus
Moscow Radio Orchestra/
  Gennady Rozhdestvensky

28 AUGUST 1966
Mahler: Symphony No 8
Heather Harper (soprano)
Gwyneth Jones (soprano)
Gwenyth Annear (soprano)
Yvonne Minton (mezzo soprano)
Norma Procter (contralto)
Vilem Pribyl (tenor)
Vladimir Ruzdjak (baritone)
Donald McIntyre (bass)
Scottish Festival Chorus
Scottish National Orchestra/
  Alexander Gibson

1967

5 SEPTEMBER 1967
Bach: Magnificat
Helen Donath (soprano)
Josephine Veasey (mezzo soprano)
Robert Tear (tenor)
Gerard Souzay (baritone)
Scottish Festival Chorus
Berlin Philharmonic Orchestra/
  Herbert von Karajan

6 SEPTEMBER 1967
Kodály: Psalmus hungaricus
Lajos Kozma (tenor)
Scottish Festival Chorus
London Symphony Orchestra/
  István Kertész

8 SEPTEMBER 1967
Stravinsky: Oedipus rex
Shirley Verrett (mezzo soprano)
Lajos Kozma (tenor)
Loren Driscoll (tenor)
Spiro Malas (baritone)
Giovanni Fojiani (bass)
Keith Michell (narrator)
Scottish Festival Chorus
London Symphony Orchestra/
  Claudio Abbado

9 SEPTEMBER 1967
Stravinsky: Symphony
  of Psalms
Vivaldi: Gloria
Verdi: Te Deum
Edda Moser (soprano)
Shirley Verrett (mezzo soprano)
Boys from George Heriot's
School, St Mary's Roman Catholic
Cathedral and Paisley Abbey
Scottish Festival Chorus
London Symphony Orchestra/
  Claudio Abbado

1968

18 AUGUST 1968
Britten: Voices for Today;
  Spring Symphony
Elly Ameling (soprano)
Helen Watts (contralto)
Peter Pears (tenor)
Scottish Festival Chorus
London Symphony Orchestra/
  István Kertész

31 AUGUST 1968
Schubert: Mass in E flat
Anne Pashley (soprano)
Sybil Michelow (mezzo soprano)
David Hughes (tenor)
Duncan Robertson (tenor)
William McCue (bass)
Scottish Festival Chorus
New Philharmonia Orchestra/
  Carlo Maria Giulini
Television recording

1 SEPTEMBER 1968
Britten: War Requiem
Galina Vishnevskaya (soprano)
Peter Pears (tenor)
Dietrich Fischer-Dieskau (baritone)
St Mary's Roman Catholic
  Cathedral boy choristers
Scottish Festival Chorus
Melos Ensemble/Benjamin Britten
New Philharmonia Orchestra/
  Carlo Maria Giulini

1969

Scottish Festival Chorus
renamed Edinburgh
Festival Chorus

24 AUGUST 1969
Berlioz: Te Deum
Britten: The Building of
  the House
John Mitchinson (tenor)
St Mary's Roman Catholic
  Cathedral boy choristers
Michael Lester-Cribb (organ)
Edinburgh Boy Singers
Edinburgh Festival Chorus
Scottish National Orchestra/Arthur
  Oldham & Alexander Gibson

30 AUGUST 1969
Debussy: Nocturnes
Ravel: Daphnis et Chloé
Edinburgh Festival Chorus
London Symphony Orchestra/
  Claudio Abbado

9 SEPTEMBER 1969
Petrassi: Magnificat
Rossini: Stabat Mater
Catherine Gayer (soprano)
Angela Gulin (soprano)
Janet Baker (mezzo soprano)
Nicolai Gedda (tenor)
Raffaele Arie (bass)
Edinburgh Festival Chorus
New Philharmonia Orchestra/
  Carlo Maria Giulini

1970

23 AUGUST 1970
Beethoven: Symphony No 9
  (Choral)
Heather Harper (soprano)
Janet Baker (mezzo soprano)
Ronald Dowd (tenor)
Raimund Herincx (bass)
Edinburgh Festival Chorus
New Philharmonia Orchestra/
  Colin Davis

27 AUGUST 1970
Beethoven: Missa solemnis
Heather Harper (soprano)
Janet Baker (mezzo soprano)
Plácido Domingo (tenor)
Robert el Hage (bass)
Edinburgh Festival Chorus
New Philharmonia Orchestra/
  Carlo Maria Giulini

12 SEPTEMBER 1970
Beethoven: Choral Fantasia
Clifford Curzon (piano)
Edinburgh Festival Chorus
Scottish National Orchestra/
  Alexander Gibson
This was the only concert at
which the EFC was asked to do an
encore: the Choral Fantasia was
repeated, minus the piano solo.

1971

21 & 22 AUGUST 1971
EIF 25th Anniversary
  Opening Concerts
National Anthem
Stravinsky: Ave Maria;
  Pater Noster
Wilson: Te Deum
Walton: Belshazzar's Feast
John Shirley-Quirk (baritone)
Edinburgh Festival Chorus
Scottish National Orchestra/
  Alexander Gibson

2 SEPTEMBER 1971
**Mozart: 'Laudate
   Dominum' from Vesperae
   solennes de confessore
Mahler: Symphony No 2
   (Resurrection)**
Margaret Price (soprano)
Janet Baker (mezzo soprano)
Edinburgh Festival Chorus
London Symphony Orchestra/
   Claudio Abbado

1972

20 AUGUST 1972
**Vaughan Williams:
   Dona nobis pacem**
Felicity Palmer (soprano)
John Carol Case (baritone)
Edinburgh Festival Chorus
Royal Philharmonic Orchestra/
   Sir Adrian Boult

29 & 30 AUGUST 1972
**Bruckner: Locus iste; Ave Maria
Brahms: Ein deutsches Requiem**
Edith Mathis (soprano)
Dietrich Fischer-Dieskau (baritone)
Edinburgh Festival Chorus
London Philharmonic Orchestra/
   Daniel Barenboim

9 September 1972
**Lutosławski: Trois poèmes
   d'Henri Michaux
Stravinsky: Symphony
   of Psalms**
Edinburgh Festival Chorus
Scottish National Orchestra/Witold
   Lutoslawski & Alexander Gibson

1973

19 AUGUST 1973
Verdi: Four Sacred Pieces
Sheila Armstrong (soprano)
Edinburgh Festival Chorus
Scottish National Orchestra/
   Alexander Gibson

23 AUGUST 1973
**Schumann: Das Paradies
   und die Peri**
Edith Mathis (soprano)
Sheila Armstrong (soprano)
Valerie Johnstone (mezzo soprano)
Delia Wallis (mezzo soprano)
Peter Pears (tenor)
Anthony Rolfe-Johnson (tenor)
Wolfgang Brendel (baritone)
Thomas Allen (baritone)
Edinburgh Festival Chorus
London Symphony Orchestra/
   Carlo Maria Giulini

27 & 28 AUGUST 1973
**Mahler: Symphony No 2
   (Resurrection)**
Sheila Armstrong (soprano)
Janet Baker (mezzo soprano)
Edinburgh Festival Chorus
London Symphony Orchestra/
   Leonard Bernstein

1 & 2 SEPTEMBER 1973
England, Ely Cathedral
**Mahler: Symphony No 2
   (Resurrection)**
Sheila Armstrong (soprano)
Janet Baker (mezzo soprano)
Edinburgh Festival Chorus
London Symphony Orchestra/
   Leonard Bernstein
Commercial recording

5 SEPTEMBER 1973
Cherubini: Requiem No 2
Edinburgh Festival
   Chorus (gentlemen)
New Philharmonia Orchestra/
   Riccardo Muti

1974

29 & 30 JANUARY 1974
*France, Théâtre des
   Champs Elysées, Paris*
Faure: Requiem
Sheila Armstrong (soprano)
Dietrich Fischer-Dieskau (baritone)
Edinburgh Festival Chorus
Orchestra de Paris/
   Daniel Barenboim

31 JANUARY 1974
France, Théâtre de la Ville, Paris
Faure: Requiem
Sheila Armstrong (soprano)
Dietrich Fischer-Dieskau (baritone)
Edinburgh Festival Chorus
Orchestra de Paris/
   Daniel Barenboim
Commercial recording

2 FEBRUARY 1974
*France, Théâtre des
   Champs Elysées, Paris*
Faure: Requiem
Sheila Armstrong (soprano)
Dietrich Fischer-Dieskau (baritone)
Edinburgh Festival Chorus
Orchestra de Paris/
   Daniel Barenboim

20 & 21 AUGUST 1974
Verdi: Requiem
Martina Arroyo (soprano) (20 Aug)
Rita Hunter (soprano) (21 Aug)
Fiorenza Cossotto (mezzo soprano)
Luciano Pavarotti (tenor)
Raffaele Arie (bass)
Edinburgh Festival Chorus
London Philharmonic Orchestra/
   Carlo Maria Giulini

25 AUGUST 1974
**Wolf: Der Feuerreiter
Bruckner: Te Deum**
Heather Harper (soprano)
Helen Watts (contralto)
Luigi Alva (tenor)
Peter Lagger (bass)
Edinburgh Festival Chorus
London Philharmonic Orchestra/
   Daniel Barenboim

7 September 1974
Ravel: Daphnis et Chloé
Edinburgh Festival Chorus
Sydney Symphony Orchestra/
   Willem van Otterloo

1975

19 JUNE 1975
France, Palais des Congrès, Paris
**Beethoven: Symphony No 9
   (Choral)**
Sona Ghazarian (soprano)
Birgit Finnila (mezzo soprano)
Dieter Ellenbeck (tenor)
Marius Rintzler (bass)
Edinburgh Festival Chorus
Orchestre de Paris/
   Daniel Barenboim

22 JUNE 1975
France, Place de la Concorde, Paris
**Beethoven: Symphony No 9
   (Choral)**
*Final movement only due
   to bad weather*
Sona Ghazarian (soprano)
Birgit Finnilä (mezzo soprano)
Dieter Ellenbeck (tenor)
Marius Rintzler (bass)
Edinburgh Festival Chorus
Orchestre de Paris/
   Daniel Barenboim
*The 100,000-strong audience was the
largest the EFC has ever performed
for. The performance was considerably
delayed due to torrential rain. The
Paris fire brigade helped out with
emergency covers and tarpaulins.*

26 & 27 AUGUST 1975
**Beethoven: Symphony No 9
   (Choral)**
Helen Donath (soprano)
Alfreda Hodgson (contralto)
Anthony Rolfe-Johnson (tenor)
Marius Rintzler (baritone)
Edinburgh Festival Chorus
London Philharmonic Orchestra/
   Carlo Maria Giulini

2 SEPTEMBER 1975
Prokofiev: Alexander Nevsky
Galina Vishnevskaya (soprano)
Edinburgh Festival Chorus
London Symphony Orchestra/
   Claudio Abbado

8 SEPTEMBER 1975
Rachmaninov: The Bells
Sheila Armstrong (soprano)
Robert Tear (tenor)
John Shirley-Quirk (baritone)
Edinburgh Festival Chorus
London Symphony Orchestra/
   André Previn

10 SEPTEMBER 1975
Bernstein: Chichester Psalms
Jeremy Maunder (treble)
Edinburgh Festival Chorus
London Symphony Orchestra/
   Leonard Bernstein
Televised performance

1976

22 AUGUST 1976
Britten: Cantata academica
Sheila Armstrong (soprano)
Helen Watts (contralto)
Anthony Rolfe-Johnson (tenor)
Thomas Allen (baritone)
Edinburgh Festival Chorus
Scottish National Orchestra/
   Mstislav Rostropovich

28 & 29 AUGUST 1976
Beethoven: Missa solemnis
Edda Moser (soprano)
Anna Reynolds (mezzo soprano)
Robert Tear (tenor)
Gwynne Howell (bass)
Edinburgh Festival Chorus
London Philharmonic Orchestra/
   Carlo Maria Giulini

7 SEPTEMBER 1976
**Beethoven: Christ on
   the Mount of Olives**
Elizabeth Harwood (soprano)
Lajos Kozma (tenor)
Gwynne Howell (bass)
Edinburgh Festival Chorus
New Philharmonia Orchestra/
   Riccardo Muti

11 SEPTEMBER 1976
Berlioz: Te Deum
Jean Dupouy (tenor)
Southend Boys Choir
Edinburgh Festival Chorus
Orchestre de Paris/
   Daniel Barenboim

1977

21 AUGUST 1977
Oldham: Psalms in Time of War
Thomas Allen (baritone)
Edinburgh Festival Chorus
Scottish National Orchestra/
   Sir Alexander Gibson

22 & 23 AUGUST 1977
Mozart: Requiem
Edith Mathis (soprano)
Helen Watts (contralto)
Robert Tear (tenor)
John Shirley-Quirk (baritone)
Edinburgh Festival Chorus
New Philharmonia Orchestra/
   Carlo Maria Giulini

9 SEPTEMBER 1977
**Stravinsky: Le roi des étoiles
Debussy: Nocturnes
Mozart: Kyrie in D minor**
Edinburgh Festival Chorus
London Symphony Orchestra/
   Claudio Abbado

Concert listings

1978

Chorus Master:
John Currie (1978–1986)

22 AUGUST 1978
Berlioz: The Damnation of Faust
Stuart Burrows (Faust)
Jessye Norman (Marguerite)
Jules Bastin (Méphistophélès)
Don Garrard (Brander)
Scottish National Orchestra
   Junior Chorus
Edinburgh Festival Chorus
London Philharmonic Orchestra/
   Daniel Barenboim

25 AUGUST 1978
Brahms: Ein deutsches Requiem
Ileana Cotrubas (soprano)
Dietrich Fischer-Dieskau (baritone)
Edinburgh Festival Chorus
London Philharmonic Orchestra/
   Carlo Maria Giulini

25 AUGUST 1978
Festival Garland Gala Concert
Late-night concert to mark the end
   of Peter Diamand's tenure as Festival
   Director with contributions from
   singers Ileana Cotrubas, Teresa
   Berganza, Dietrich Fischer-Dieskau
   and Jessye Norman, plus Cathy Gayer
   (cabaret songs), Isaac Stern (violin)
   and Daniel Barenboim (piano).
Edinburgh Festival Chorus
   (Mozart: Ave Verum Corpus)
London Philharmonic Orchestra/
   Claudio Abbado, Daniel Barenboim,
   John Currie & Sir Alexander
   Gibson (conductors)

26 AUGUST 1978
Brahms: Ein deutsches Requiem
Ileana Cotrubas (soprano)
Dietrich Fischer-Dieskau (baritone)
Edinburgh Festival Chorus
London Philharmonic Orchestra/
   Carlo Maria Giulini

9 SEPTEMBER 1978
Janáček: Glagolitic Mass
Dvořák: Te Deum
Wendy Fine (soprano)
Anne Collins (contralto)
Vilem Pribyl (tenor)
John Shirley-Quirk (bass)
Edinburgh Festival Chorus
Scottish National Orchestra/
   Sir Alexander Gibson

1979

Festival Director:
John Drummond (1979–1983)

20 AUGUST 1979
Britten: Spring Symphony
Margaret Marshall (soprano)
Helen Watts (contralto)
Sir Peter Pears (tenor)
Scottish National Orchestra
   Junior Chorus
Edinburgh Festival Chorus
BBC Symphony Orchestra/
   Gennadi Rozhdestvensky

22 AUGUST 1979
Mahler: Symphony No 3
Lucia Valentini-Terrani
   (mezzo soprano)
Scottish National Orchestra
   Junior Chorus
Edinburgh Festival Chorus (ladies)
London Symphony Orchestra/
   Claudio Abbado

4 SEPTEMBER 1979
Walton: Belshazzar's Feast
Benjamin Luxon (baritone)
Edinburgh Festival Chorus
Hallé Orchestra/James Loughran

8 September 1979
Ravel: Daphnis et Chloé
Edinburgh Festival Chorus
Boston Symphony Orchestra/
   Seiji Ozawa

1980

17 AUGUST 1980
Beethoven: Choral Fantasia
Peter Frankl (piano)
Edinburgh Festival Chorus
Philharmonia Orchestra/
   Riccardo Muti

19 AUGUST 1980
Tippett: A Child of Our Time
Jessye Norman (soprano)
Alfreda Hodgson (mezzo soprano)
Robert Tear (tenor)
Norman Bailey (baritone)
Edinburgh Festival Chorus
Scottish National Orchestra/
   Sir Alexander Gibson

27 AUGUST 1980
Haydn: The Creation
Helen Donath (soprano)
David Rendall (tenor)
Gwynne Howell (bass)
Edinburgh Festival Chorus
London Philharmonic Orchestra/
   Jesús López-Cobos

2 SEPTEMBER 1980
Orff: Carmina Burana
Sheila Armstrong (soprano)
John van Kesteren (tenor)
Håkan Hagegård (baritone)
Scottish National Orchestra
   Junior Chorus
Edinburgh Festival Chorus
London Symphony Orchestra/
   John Pritchard

6 SEPTEMBER 1980
Berlioz: Te Deum
Debussy: Nocturnes
Philip Langridge (tenor)
Scottish National Orchestra
   Junior Chorus
Edinburgh Festival Chorus
London Symphony Orchestra/
   Claudio Abbado

1981

16 & 18 AUGUST 1981
Bach: St Matthew Passion
Margaret Price (soprano)
Jessye Norman (soprano)
Peter Schreier (tenor)
Philip Langridge (tenor)
Hermann Prey (baritone)
Gwynne Howell (bass)
Scottish National Orchestra
   Junior Chorus
Edinburgh Festival Chorus
London Symphony Orchestra/
   Claudio Abbado

26 AUGUST 1981
Verdi: Stabat Mater;
Te Deum
Edinburgh Festival Chorus
London Philharmonic Orchestra/
   Riccardo Chailly

29 AUGUST 1981
Berlioz: Roméo et Juliette
Julia Hamari (soprano)
Lajos Kozma (tenor)
John Paul Bogart (bass)
Edinburgh Festival Chorus
Philharmonia Orchestra/
   Riccardo Muti

1 SEPTEMBER 1981
Stravinsky: Le roi des étoiles
Mahler: Symphony No 2
   (Resurrection)
Jill Gomez (soprano)
Alfreda Hodgson (contralto)
Edinburgh Festival Chorus
Philharmonia Orchestra/
   Simon Rattle

3 SEPTEMBER 1981
Bruckner: Ecce sacerdos; Ave
   Maria; Christus factus est
Bartók: Four Hungarian
   Folksongs
Oliver: Namings
Poulenc: Folksongs
Tallis: Spem in alium
Verdi: Ave Maria; Laudi alla
   Vergine; Pater noster
Edinburgh Festival Chorus
Equale Brass/John Currie

5 SEPTEMBER 1981
Vaughan Williams: Serenade
   to Music
Bruckner: Te Deum
Felicity Lott (soprano)
Penelope Walker (mezzo soprano)
John Mitchinson (tenor)
Marius Rintzler (bass)
Edinburgh Festival Chorus
Scottish National Orchestra/
   Sir Alexander Gibson

29 NOVEMBER 1981
London, Royal Festival Hall
Berlioz: Roméo et Juliette
Julia Hamari (soprano)
Robert Tear (tenor)
John Paul Bogart (baritone)
Edinburgh Festival Chorus
Philharmonia Orchestra/
   Riccardo Muti

27 DECEMBER 1981
Israel, Jerusalem Theatre, Jerusalem
Handel: Israel in Egypt
Irene Drummond (soprano)
Llyndall Trotman (soprano)
Christine Cairns (mezzo soprano)
Stewart Patterson (tenor)
John Hearne (baritone)
Stephen Roberts (bass)
Scottish National Orchestra Chorus
Edinburgh Festival Chorus
Jerusalem Symphony Orchestra/
   John Currie

29 DECEMBER 1981
Israel, Jerusalem Theatre, Jerusalem
Seter: Jerusalem Symphony
Walton: Belshazzar's Feast
Stephen Roberts (baritone)
Scottish National Orchestra Chorus
John Currie Singers
Edinburgh Festival Chorus
Jerusalem Symphony Orchestra/
   Gary Bertini

1982

3 JANUARY1982
Israel, Binyanei HaUma
   Concert Hall, Jerusalem
Berlioz: Grande messe des morts
Keith Lewis (tenor)
Scottish National Orchestra Chorus
John Currie Singers
Edinburgh Festival Chorus
Jerusalem Symphony Orchestra/
   Gary Bertini

4 JANUARY 1982
Israel, On Top of a Red Rock, Eilat
Handel: Israel in Egypt
Irene Drummond (soprano)
Llyndall Trotman (soprano)
Christine Cairns (mezzo soprano)
Stewart Patterson (tenor)
John Hearne (baritone)
Stephen Roberts (bass)
John Currie Singers
Scottish National Orchestra Chorus
Edinburgh Festival Chorus
Jerusalem Symphony Orchestra/
 John Currie
Televised broadcast and recording

22 & 24 AUGUST 1982
Verdi: Requiem
Margaret Price (soprano)
Jessye Norman (soprano)
José Carreras (tenor)
Ruggero Raimondi (bass)
Edinburgh Festival Chorus
London Symphony Orchestra/
 Claudio Abbado

3 SEPTEMBER 1982
Fauré: Requiem
Jennifer Smith (soprano)
Dale Duesing (baritone)
Edinburgh Festival Chorus
Philharmonia Orchestra/
 Simon Rattle

5 SEPTEMBER 1982
Mahler: Symphony No 3
Faith Wilson (mezzo soprano)
Scottish National Orchestra
 Junior Chorus
Edinburgh Festival Chorus (ladies)
London Philharmonic Orchestra/
 Sir Georg Solti

8 SEPTEMBER 1982
Beethoven: Missa solemnis
Helen Donath (soprano)
Doris Soffel (contralto)
Siegfried Jerusalem (tenor)
Hans Sotin (bass)
Edinburgh Festival Chorus
London Philharmonic Orchestra/
 Sir Georg Solti

10 SEPTEMBER 1982
London, Royal Albert Hall
Beethoven: Missa solemnis
Helen Donath (soprano)
Doris Soffel (contralto)
Siegfried Jerusalem (tenor)
Hans Sotin (bass)
Edinburgh Festival Chorus
London Philharmonic Orchestra/
 Sir Georg Solti
Televised broadcast

1983

21 AUGUST 1983
**Beethoven: Symphony No 9
 (Choral)**
Linda Esther Gray (soprano)
Carolyn Watkinson (mezzo soprano)
John Mitchinson (tenor)
Robert Lloyd (bass)
Edinburgh Festival Chorus
Philharmonia Orchestra/
 Andrew Davis

24 AUGUST 1983
Wagner: Lohengrin, Act 2
Rosalind Plowright (Elsa)
Eva Randová (Ortrud)
Siegfried Jerusalem (Lohengrin)
Sergei Leiferkus (Telramund)
Hartmut Welker (Telramund)
Siegfried Lorenz (Herald)
Robert Lloyd (King Henry)
Edinburgh Festival Chorus
London Symphony Orchestra/
 Claudio Abbado

4 SEPTEMBER 1983
Schoenberg: Gurrelieder
Marilyn Zschau (Tove)
Ann Murray (Wood Dove)
Jon Frederic West (Waldemar)
Philip Langridge (Klaus the Fool)
Nikolaus Hillebrand (Peasant)
Hans Hotter (Narrator)
Edinburgh Festival Chorus
Scottish National Orchestra/
 Sir Alexander Gibson

8 SEPTEMBER 1983
Bruckner: Mass in F minor
Margaret Marshall (soprano)
Florence Quivar (mezzo soprano)
Graham Clark (tenor)
Gwynne Howell (bass)
Edinburgh Festival Chorus
Scottish National Orchestra/
 Jesús López-Cobos

1984

**Festival Director:
Frank Dunlop (1984–1991)**

12 AUGUST 1984
Rossini: Stabat Mater
Cecilia Gasdia (soprano)
Ann Murray (mezzo soprano)
Francisco Araiza (tenor)
James Morris (bass)
Edinburgh Festival Chorus
Philharmonia Orchestra/
 Riccardo Muti

18 AUGUST 1984
Prokofiev: Alexander Nevsky
Irina Arkhipova (mezzo soprano)
Edinburgh Festival Chorus
Royal Philharmonic Orchestra/
 Yuri Temirkanov

21 AUGUST 1984
**Parry: Blest Pair of Sirens
Vaughan Williams:
 A Sea Symphony**
Felicity Lott (soprano)
Stephen Roberts (baritone)
Edinburgh Festival Chorus
Scottish National Orchestra/
 Neeme Järvi

25 AUGUST 1984
Holst: The Planets
Edinburgh Festival Chorus (ladies)
Australian Youth Orchestra/
 Sir Charles Mackerras

28 AUGUST 1984
Mozart: Mass in C
Edith Mathis (soprano)
Carolyn Watkinson (mezzo soprano)
Philip Langridge (tenor)
John Shirley-Quirk (baritone)
Edinburgh Festival Chorus
London Symphony Orchestra/
 Rafael Kubelík

1 SEPTEMBER 1984
Delius: A Mass of Life
Heather Harper (soprano)
Sarah Walker (mezzo soprano)
Philip Langridge (tenor)
Jonathan Summers (baritone)
Edinburgh Festival Chorus
Scottish National Orchestra/
 Sir Charles Mackerras

11 OCTOBER 1984
Germany, Lukaskirche, Munich
**Fauré: Requiem
Parry: Blest Pair of Sirens**
Edinburgh Festival Chorus
Graunke Symphony Orchestra/
 John Currie

1985

11 AUGUST 1985
**Britten: National Anthem
Berlioz: La Marseillaise
Ravel: Daphnis et Chloé**
Edinburgh Festival Chorus
Orchestre National de France/
 Charles Dutoit

17 AUGUST 1985
Mahler: Symphony No 8
Jill Gomez (soprano)
Suzanne Murphy (soprano)
Rosa Mannion (soprano)
Alfreda Hodgson (mezzo soprano)
Anne Collins (contralto)
John Mitchinson (tenor)
Thomas Hampson (baritone)
Stafford Dean (bass)
Scottish National Orchestra
 Junior Chorus
Edinburgh Festival Chorus
Scottish National Orchestra/
 Neeme Järvi

20 AUGUST 1985
**Schumann: Das Paradies
und die Peri**
Pamela Coburn (The Peri)
Brenda Boozer (The Angel)
Neil Jenkins (The Young Man)
Catherine Dubosc (The Young Girl)
Thomas Hampson (Gazna)
Neil Rosenshein (Narrator)
Edinburgh Festival Chorus
Orchestre de l'Opéra De Lyon/
 John Eliot Gardiner

29 August 1985
**Mahler: Symphony No 2
 (Resurrection)**
Lucia Popp (soprano)
Carolyn Watkinson (mezzo soprano)
Edinburgh Festival Chorus
Philharmonia Orchestra/
 Giuseppe Sinopoli

1986

10, 12 & 14 August 1986
Weber: Oberon
Philip Langridge (Oberon)
Gail Rolfe (Titania)
James Robertson (Puck)
Peter Birch (Son of Charlemagne)
Paul Frey (Sir Huon of Bordeaux)
Benjamin Luxon (Sherasmin)
Elizabeth Connell (Reiza)
La Verne Williams (Fatima)
Robert Oates (Haroun el
 Raschid/Abdallah)
Peter Birch (Babekan)
Edinburgh Festival Chorus
Junge Deutsche Philharmonie/
 Seiji Ozawa

16 & 18 AUGUST 1986
Germany, Die Alte Oper, Frankfurt
Weber: Oberon
Philip Langridge (Oberon)
Gail Rolfe (Titania)
James Robertson (Puck)
Peter Birch (Son of Charlemagne)
Paul Frey (Sir Huon of Bordeaux)
Benjamin Luxon (Sherasmin)
Elizabeth Connell (Reiza)
La Verne Williams (Fatima)
Robert Oates (Haroun el
 Raschid/Abdallah)
Peter Birch (Babekan)
Edinburgh Festival Chorus
Junge Deutsche Philharmonie/
 Seiji Ozawa
Television broadcast

17 AUGUST 1986
**Lesueur: Ossian's Dream
Méhul: Uthal**
Pamela Myers (Malvina)
Jeffrey Talbot (Uthal)
Mark Curtis (Ullin)
Anthony Michaels-Moore (Chief Bard)
Roderick Earle (Larmor)
James Cairncross (Narrator)
Edinburgh Festival Chorus
Scottish National Orchestra/
 Neeme Järvi

24 AUGUST 1986
**EIF 40th Anniversary
Gala Concert**
Verdi: Sanctus from Requiem
Weber: 'Hail to the Knight'
  from Oberon
Lloyd-Webber: Joseph and
  the Amazing Technicolor
  Dreamcoat (excerpts)
Scottish songs, readings, jazz, dance
Introductions by Sean Connery,
  Denise Coffey & Hannah Gordon
Felicity Lott & Joyce Fieldsend –
  Oberon
Ian Charleson – Richard II
Cleo Laine & John Dankworth
  – Eight songs
Readings by Tom Fleming,
  Bernard Bresslaw, Denise Coffey
  & Paul Rogers
Tim Rice & Gary Bond – Joseph and
  his Amazing Technicolor Dreamcoat
Leanne Benjamin & David Yow –
  Sadler's Wells Royal Ballet
Leonard Friedman – playing
  Hogg's violin
Royal Scottish Academy
  of Music and Drama
National Youth Music Theatre
Edinburgh Festival Chorus
Hallé Orchestra/John Currie,
  John Dankworth, Bramwell Tovey
  & Stanisław Skrowaczewski

28 AUGUST 1986
Stravinsky: Oedipus rex
Alfreda Hodgson (contralto)
Robert Tear (tenor)
Maldwyn Davies (tenor)
Anthony Michaels-Moore (baritone)
Stafford Dean (bass-baritone)
John Neville (narrator)
Edinburgh Festival Chorus
Toronto Symphony Orchestra/
  Andrew Davis

29 AUGUST 1986
Elgar: The Dream of Gerontius
Janet Baker (mezzo soprano)
John Mitchinson (tenor)
John Shirley-Quirk (baritone)
Edinburgh Festival Chorus
City of Birmingham Symphony
  Orchestra/Simon Rattle

30 AUGUST 1986
**Mahler: Symphony No 2
(Resurrection)**
Felicity Lott (soprano)
Janet Baker (mezzo soprano)
Edinburgh Festival Chorus
City of Birmingham Symphony
  Orchestra/Simon Rattle

7 SEPTEMBER 1986
London, Royal Albert Hall
**Mahler: Symphony No 5
Verdi: Four Sacred Pieces**
Edinburgh Festival Chorus
BBC Symphony Orchestra/
  Marek Janowski
BBC Radio 3 broadcast

1987

**Chorus Master:
Arthur Oldham (1987–1994)**

13 AUGUST 1987
Berlioz: The Damnation of Faust
Ann Murray (Marguerite)
David Rendall (Faust)
David Wilson-Johnson
  (Méphistophélès)
Stephen Richardson (Brander)
Fiona Wright (EFC) (Voix Céleste)
Edinburgh Festival Chorus
Scottish National Orchestra/
  Neeme Järvi
Televised broadcast

17 AUGUST 1987
**Bruckner: Locus iste; Ave Maria;
Afferentur regi; Tota pulchra;
Virga Jesse; Os justi; Christus
factus est; Ecce sacerdos**
Edinburgh Festival Chorus
The Wallace Collection/
  Arthur Oldham

21 AUGUST 1987
**Britten: National Anthem
Beethoven: Symphony No 9
(Choral)**
Mechthild Gessendorf (soprano)
Linda Finnie (mezzo soprano)
Richard Leech (tenor)
Peter Meven (bass)
Edinburgh Festival Chorus
Pittsburgh Symphony Orchestra/
  Lorin Maazel

26 AUGUST 1987
Bernstein: Chichester Psalms
David Stout (treble)
Edinburgh Festival Chorus
Pittsburgh Symphony Orchestra/
  Michael Tilson Thomas

25 SEPTEMBER 1987
*France, La Côte St André (home
  town of Hector Berlioz)*
Berlioz: The Damnation of Faust
Diana Montague (Marguerite)
Michael Myers (Faust)
Pierre Thau (Méphistophélès)
René Schirrer (Brander)
Fiona Wright (EFC) (Voix Céleste)
Edinburgh Festival Chorus
Orchestre de l'Opéra de Lyon/
  John Eliot Gardiner

27 & 30 SEPTEMBER 1987
*France, Auditorium
  Maurice Ravel, Lyon*
Berlioz: The Damnation of Faust
Anne Sophie von Otter (Marguerite)
Michael Myers (Faust)
Jean-Philippe Lafont (Méphistophélès)
Rene Schirrer (Brander)
Fiona Wright (EFC) (Voix Céleste)
Edinburgh Festival Chorus
Orchestre de l'Opéra de Lyon/
  John Eliot Gardiner
Commercial recording

1988

14 AUGUST 1988
Orff: Carmina Burana
Juliet Booth (soprano)
Neil Archer (tenor)
Sergei Leiferkus (baritone)
St Mary's Roman Catholic
  Cathedral boy choristers
Edinburgh Festival Chorus
Scottish National Orchestra/
  Neeme Järvi
Televised broadcast

21 AUGUST 1988
**Stravinsky: Symphony
of Psalms**
Edinburgh Festival Chorus
Swedish Radio Symphony
  Orchestra/Esa-Pekka Salonen

26 AUGUST 1988
**Bruckner: Mass in E minor
Schubert: Der Gondelfahrer;
  Frühlingsgesang;
  Nachtgesang im Walde
Brahms: Four Songs Op 17
Oldham: In Praise of the Virgin**
Linda Towers (EFC) (mezzo soprano)
Michael Lester-Cribb (piano)
Edinburgh Festival Chorus
Scottish Chamber Orchestra/
  Arthur Oldham

1 & 3 SEPTEMBER 1988
Verdi: Requiem
Susan Dunn (soprano)
Stefania Toczyska (mezzo soprano)
Tonio Di Paolo (tenor)
Gwynne Howell (bass)
Edinburgh Festival Chorus
Orchestra of the Maggio Musicale
  Fiorentino/James Conlon

1989

12 FEBRUARY 1989
Glasgow, Theatre Royal
**Lockerbie Memorial Concert
  In the presence of HRH
  the Duke and Duchess
  of Gloucester
Verdi: Requiem**
Jane Eaglen (soprano)
Linda Finnie (mezzo soprano)
Jorge Pita (tenor)
Willard White (bass)
Edinburgh Festival Chorus
Orchestra of Scottish Opera/
  John Mauceri

12 & 13 AUGUST 1989
Falla: Atlántida; La vida breve
Maria Oran (soprano)
Alicia Nafe (mezzo soprano)
Paloma Pérez-Iñigo (mezzo soprano)
Josep Ruiz (tenor)
Jorge Anton (tenor)
Enrique Baquerizo (baritone)
Jesus Sainz Remiro (bass-baritone)
Lucero Tena (dancer)
Gabriel Moreno (flamenco singer)
Carmelo Martinez (guitar)
Edinburgh Festival Chorus
National Orchestra of Spain/
  Rafael Frühbeck de Burgos

22 AUGUST 1989
Haydn: The Creation
Arleen Augér (soprano)
Philip Langridge (tenor)
Benjamin Luxon (baritone)
Edinburgh Festival Chorus
City of Birmingham Symphony
  Orchestra/Simon Rattle

28 AUGUST 1989
**Berlioz: La Marseillaise
Cherubini: Requiem**
Edinburgh Festival Chorus
Nouvel Orchestre Philharmonique/
  Marek Janowski
Broadcast live on French radio

2 & 3 SEPTEMBER 1989
Berlioz: Grande messe des morts
Martyn Hill (tenor)
Edinburgh Festival Chorus
BBC Scottish Symphony Orchestra/
  Rafael Frühbeck de Burgos

1990

22 JUNE 1990
France, Basilique de Saint-Denis, Paris
Dvořák: Requiem
Gabriela Beňačková (soprano)
Stefania Toxzyska (mezzo soprano)
Dennis O'Neill (tenor)
Gwynne Howell (bass)
Edinburgh Festival Chorus
Rotterdam Philharmonic Orchestra/
  James Conlon

24 JUNE 1990
France, Chapelle du Lycée, Rouen
Prokofiev: Alexander Nevsky
Evgenia Gorokhovskaia
  (mezzo soprano)
Edinburgh Festival Chorus
Leningrad Philharmonic Orchestra/
  Yuri Temirkanov

25 JUNE 1990
France, Basilique de Saint-Denis, Paris
Prokofiev: Alexander Nevsky
Evgenia Gorokhovskaia
  (mezzo soprano)
Edinburgh Festival Chorus
Leningrad Philharmonic Orchestra/
  Yuri Temirkanov

13 AUGUST 1990
Martinů: The Greek Passion
Christine Bunning (soprano)
Phyllis Cannan (soprano)
Beverley Mills (mezzo soprano)
Morag Watson (EFC) (mezzo soprano)
Neville Ackerman (tenor)
Arthur Davies (tenor)
John Harris (tenor)
Jeffrey Lawton (tenor)
Alan Woodrow (tenor)
John Hancorn (baritone)
David Gwynne (bass-baritone)
Stephen Richardson (bass-baritone)
Geoffrey Moses (bass)
Edinburgh Festival Chorus
Prague Symphony Orchestra/
Jiří Bělohlávek

20 AUGUST 1990
**Grainger: Songs for soloists
and chorus**
Lynton Atkinson (tenor)
Richard Jackson (baritone)
Edinburgh Festival Chorus
City of London Sinfonia/
Richard Hickox

21 AUGUST 1990
Prokofiev: Alexander Nevsky
Elena Zaremba (mezzo soprano)
Edinburgh Festival Chorus
Orchestra of the Bolshoi
Theatre/Alexander Lazarev

26 AUGUST 1990
Dvořák: Requiem
Carolyn James (soprano)
Alexandra Milcheva (mezzo soprano)
Vinson Cole (tenor)
Gwynne Howell (bass)
Edinburgh Festival Chorus
Rotterdam Philharmonic Orchestra/
James Conlon

1 & 2 SEPTEMBER 1990
Brahms: Ein deutsches Requiem
Arleen Augér (soprano)
Thomas Allen (baritone)
Edinburgh Festival Chorus
Berlin Symphony Orchestra/
Claus Peter Flor

7 DECEMBER 1990
Glasgow, Royal Concert Hall
**Mahler: Symphony No 2
(Resurrection)**
Yvonne Kenny (soprano)
Sarah Walker (mezzo soprano)
Edinburgh Festival Chorus
BBC Scottish Symphony Orchestra/
Leopold Hager

1991

11 AUGUST 1991
Mozart: Mass in C minor
Eileen Hulse (soprano)
Adrianne Pieczonka (soprano)
Andrew Tusa (tenor)
Johannes Mannov (bass)
Edinburgh Festival Chorus
Scottish Chamber Orchestra/
Yehudi Menuhin

14 AUGUST 1991
Britten: War Requiem
Galina Simkina (soprano)
David Rendall (tenor)
Willard White (bass)
Royal Scottish Orchestra
Junior Chorus
Edinburgh Festival Chorus
Royal Scottish Orchestra/
Sir Alexander Gibson

20 AUGUST 1991
Mozart: Requiem
Tatiana Novikova (soprano)
Evgenia Gorokhovskaya
(mezzo soprano)
Alexei Martinov (tenor)
Sergei Leiferkus (baritone)
Edinburgh Festival Chorus
Leningrad Philharmonic
Orchestra/Yuri Temirkanov
*This concert took place on the day
hardline Soviet leaders attempted
a coup and imprisoned Mikhail
Gorbachev, causing not only an
emotionally charged performance but
also deep distress and uncertainty
for the Russian musicians.*

28 AUGUST 1991
Janáček: Glagolitic Mass
Zora Jehličková (soprano)
Eva Randová (mezzo soprano)
Leo Marian Vodička (tenor)
Peter Mikuláš (tenor)
Jaroslav Tvrzský (organ)
Edinburgh Festival Chorus
Czech Philharmonic Orchestra/
Sir Charles Mackerras

1992

**Festival Director:
Brian McMaster (1992–2006)**

16 APRIL 1992
Dundee, Caird Hall
Brahms: Ein deutsches Requiem
Lorna Anderson (soprano)
Donald Maxwell (baritone)
Edinburgh Festival Chorus
BBC Scottish Symphony Orchestra/
Leopold Hager

17 APRIL 1992
Glasgow, Royal Concert Hall
Brahms: Ein deutsches Requiem
Lorna Anderson (soprano)
Donald Maxwell (baritone)
Edinburgh Festival Chorus
BBC Scottish Symphony Orchestra/
Leopold Hager

16 AUGUST 1992
Schoenberg: Moses and Aaron
William Cochran (Aaron)
Willard White (Moses)
Rebecca Evans (Young Girl/
Naked Virgin)
Paul Charles Clarke (Young Man/
Naked Youth)
Jonathan Best (Ephraimite/A Man)
Alastair Miles (Priest)
Soloists from EFC
Cappella Nova
Edinburgh Festival Chorus
BBC Scottish Symphony Orchestra/
Richard Armstrong

24 & 25 AUGUST 1992
Edinburgh, St Giles' Cathedral
**Tchaikovsky: Liturgy of
St John Chrysostom**
Edinburgh Festival Chorus/
Arthur Oldham

3 SEPTEMBER 1992
Tchaikovsky: Moscow Cantata
Olga Borodina (mezzo soprano)
Dmitri Kharitonov (baritone)
Edinburgh Festival Chorus
Royal Scottish Orchestra/
Yuri Simonov

4 DECEMBER 1992
Glasgow, Royal Concert Hall
**Beethoven: Symphony No 9
(Choral)**
Janice Cairns (soprano)
Jean Rigby (mezzo soprano)
Robert Tear (tenor)
John Connell (bass)
Edinburgh Festival Chorus
BBC Scottish Symphony Orchestra/
Mark Wigglesworth

10 DECEMBER 1992
**Euro Summit Gala Concert,
Usher Hall, Edinburgh
In the presence of
HRH Princess Margaret
Jacob: The National Anthem
Handel: Music for the
Royal Fireworks
MacMillan: Tryst
Poulenc: Gloria
Beethoven: 'Ode to Joy' from
Symphony No 9 (Choral)**
Lillian Watson (soprano)
72 European dancers
Scottish Chamber Orchestra Chorus
Edinburgh Festival Chorus
Scottish Chamber Orchestra/
Hans Vonk
Live BBC Scotland television broadcast

1993

15 AUGUST 1993
**Janáček: Amarus
Schubert: Mass No 5**
Stefan Margita (tenor)
Yvonne Kenny (soprano)
Fiona Janes (mezzo soprano)
John Mark Ainsley (tenor)
Andreas Schmidt (bass)
Edinburgh Festival Chorus
Royal Scottish National Orchestra/
Walter Weller

16 AUGUST 1993
Mozart: Così fan tutte
Felicity Lott (Fiordiligi)
Marie McLaughlin (Dorabella)
Nuccia Focile (Despina)
Jerry Hadley (Ferrando)
Alessandro Corbelli (Guglielmo)
Gilles Cachemaille (Don Alfonso)
Edinburgh Festival Chorus
Scottish Chamber Orchestra/
Sir Charles Mackerras
Commercial recording

26 AUGUST 1993
**Verdi: Oberto, Conte
di San Bonifacio**
Maria Guleghina (Leonora)
Jane Henschel (Cuniza)
Fiona Kimm (Imelda)
Alastair Miles (Oberto,
Conte di San Bonifacio)
Dennis O'Neill (Riccardo,
Conte di Salinguerra)
Edinburgh Festival Chorus
Royal Scottish National Orchestra/
David Robertson

29 AUGUST 1993
Verdi: Requiem
Jane Eaglen (soprano)
Olga Borodina (mezzo soprano)
Dennis O'Neill (tenor)
Alastair Miles (bass)
Edinburgh Festival Chorus
Royal Scottish National Orchestra/
Carlo Rizzi

3 SEPTEMBER 1993
Schubert: Mass No 6
Dawn Upshaw (soprano)
Patricia Bardon (mezzo soprano)
John Mark Ainsley (tenor)
Philip Salmon (tenor)
Alastair Miles (bass)
Edinburgh Festival Chorus
Orchestra of Scottish Opera/
Richard Armstrong

Concert listings

1994

14 AUGUST 1994
Mahler: Symphony No 8
Janice Watson (soprano)
Jane Eaglen (soprano)
Susan Chilcott (soprano)
Catherine Keen (mezzo soprano)
Patrician Bardon (mezzo soprano)
Peter Svensson (tenor)
Gregory Yurisich (baritone)
Gwynne Howell (bass)
Royal Scottish National
   Orchestra Junior Chorus
Edinburgh Festival Chorus
Royal Scottish National Orchestra/
   Donald Runnicles

17 AUGUST 1994
Beethoven: Leonora
Janice Watson (Leonore)
William Kendall (Florestan)
Rebecca Evans (Marzelline)
Paul Charles Clarke (Jacquino)
Donald Maxwell (Pizarro)
Franz Hawlata (Rocco)
Neal Davies (Don Fernando)
Ivor Klayman (EFC) (First Prisoner)
William Durran (EFC)
(Second Prisoner)
Edinburgh Festival Chorus
Scottish Chamber Orchestra/
   Sir Charles Mackerras

31 AUGUST 1994
**Schumann: Scenes
   from Goethe's Faust**
Susan Gritton (soprano)
Anne Dawson (soprano)
Alwyn Mellor (soprano)
Anne Taylor-Morley (soprano)
Catherine Denley (mezzo soprano)
Rufus Müller (tenor)
Boje Skovhus (baritone)
Neal Davies (bass)
Alastair Miles (bass)
Royal Scottish National
Orchestra Junior Chorus
Edinburgh Festival Chorus
London Philharmonic Orchestra/
   John Nelson

3 SEPTEMBER 1994
Elgar: The Dream of Gerontius
Ann Murray (mezzo soprano)
Philip Langridge (tenor)
Alastair Miles (bass)
Edinburgh Festival Chorus
Royal Scottish National Orchestra/
   Sir Charles Mackerras

1995

**Chorus Master:
David Jones (1995–2007)**

**30th Anniversary of the
Edinburgh Festival Chorus**
*The EFC gave 11 concerts, including
five Usher Hall concerts during the
Edinburgh International Festival, one
concert at the BBC Proms in London,
and performances of Zimmermann's
'Requiem for a Young Poet' in five
major European cities. The EFC
spent a week in Salzburg in March,
making a commercial recording
of the work and a documentary
was filmed by WDR, West German
Broadcasting Cologne, in September.*

12 MARCH 1995
*Austria, Grosses Festspielhaus,
   Salzburg*
**Zimmermann: Requiem
   for a Young Poet**
Vlatka Orsanic (soprano)
James Johnson (baritone)
Bernhard Schir (speaker)
Michael Rotschopf (speaker)
Christoph Grund (organ)
Kölner Rundfunkchor
Südfunkchor, Stuttgart
Slovakian Philharmonic Chorus,
   Bratislava
Bratislava City Chorus
Edinburgh Festival Chorus
Alexander von Schlippenbach
Jazz Combo
SWF-Sinfonieorchester, Baden-
   Baden/Michael Gielen
Commercial recording

14 MARCH 1995
Germany, Konzerthaus, Berlin
**Zimmermann: Requiem
   for a Young Poet**
Same forces as above
Live broadcast on German radio

13 AUGUST 1995
Bruckner: Te Deum
Jane Eaglen (soprano)
Liliana Nichiteanu (mezzo soprano)
Endrik Wottrich (tenor)
Robert Lloyd (bass)
Edinburgh Festival Chorus
Gustav Mahler Jugendorchester/
   Claudio Abbado

15 AUGUST 1995
Dvořák: Stabat Mater
Judith Howarth (soprano)
Anne Sofie von Otter (mezzo soprano)
Anthony Rolfe Johnson (tenor)
Alastair Miles (bass)
Edinburgh Festival Chorus
Philharmonia Orchestra/
   John Eliot Gardiner

19 AUGUST 1995
Dvořák: Requiem
Jane Eaglen (soprano)
Randi Stene (mezzo soprano)
Thomas Moser (tenor)
Alastair Miles (bass)
Edinburgh Festival Chorus
Royal Scottish National Orchestra/
   Sir Charles Mackerras

24 AUGUST 1995
Wagner: Siegfried, Act 2
**Wagner: Götterdämmerung,
   Act 3**
Jane Eaglen (soprano)
Susan Chilcott (soprano)
Janice Watson (soprano)
Jane Irwin (mezzo soprano)
Philip Joll (bass-baritone)
John Tranter (bass)
Edinburgh Festival Chorus
Royal Scottish National Orchestra/
   Donald Runnicles

29 AUGUST 1995
**Zimmermann: Requiem
   for a Young Poet**
Vlatka Orsanic (soprano)
James Johnson (baritone)
Bernhard Schir (speaker)
Michael Rotschopf (speaker)
Christoph Grund (organ)
Kölner Rundfunkchor
Südfunkchor, Stuttgart
Slovakian Philharmonic Chorus,
   Bratislava
Bratislava City Chorus
Edinburgh Festival Chorus
Alexander von Schlippenbach
Jazz Combo
SWF-Sinfonieorchester, Baden-
   Baden/Michael Gielen

1 SEPTEMBER 1995
*Austria, Grosses Festspielhaus,
   Salzburg*
**Zimmermann: Requiem
   for a Young Poet**
Forces as in 29 August
Edinburgh performance

15 SEPTEMBER 1995
London, Royal Albert Hall
**Mahler: Symphony No 2
   (Resurrection)**
Rosa Mannion (soprano)
Jean Rigby (mezzo soprano)
BBC Singers
Brighton Festival Chorus
Edinburgh Festival Chorus
BBC Philharmonic Orchestra/
   Sir Charles Mackerras

19 AUGUST 1995
Dvořák: Requiem
Jane Eaglen (soprano)
Randi Stene (mezzo soprano)
Thomas Moser (tenor)
Alastair Miles (bass)
Edinburgh Festival Chorus
Royal Scottish National Orchestra/
   Sir Charles Mackerras

21 SEPTEMBER 1995
France, Théâtre du Châtelet, Paris
**Zimmermann: Requiem
   for a Young Poet**
Vlatka Orsanic (soprano)
James Johnson (baritone)
Bernhard Schir (speaker)
Karl Rudolf Menke (speaker)
Christoph Grund (organ)
Kölner Rundfunkchor
Südfunkchor, Stuttgart
Slovakian Philharmonic Chorus,
   Bratislava
Bratislava City Chorus
Edinburgh Festival Chorus
Alexander von Schlippenbach
Jazz Combo
SWF-Sinfonieorchester, Baden-
   Baden/Michael Gielen

23 SEPTEMBER 1995
Germany, Philharmonie Hall, Cologne
**Zimmermann: Requiem
   for a Young Poet**
Forces as in 21 September
Paris performance

1996

11 AUGUST 1996
**Beethoven: Symphony No 9
   (Choral)**
**Schoenberg: A Survivor
   from Warsaw**
Hillevi Martinpelto (soprano)
Jane Irwin (mezzo soprano)
Heinz Kruse (tenor)
Bryn Terfel (baritone)
Olaf Bär (narrator)
Edinburgh Festival Chorus
Royal Scottish National Orchestra/
   Donald Runnicles

12 AUGUST 1996
Beethoven: Fidelio
Anne Evans (Leonore)
Ildiko Raimondi (Marzelline)
John Mark Ainsley (Jaquino)
Heinz Kruse (Florestan)
Franz-Josef Kapellmann (Don Pizzaro)
Siegfried Vogel (Rocco)
David Wilson-Johnson (Don Fernando)
Edinburgh Festival Chorus
Scottish Chamber Orchestra/
   Sir Charles Mackerras
Commercial recording

19 AUGUST 1996
Britten: War Requiem
Elena Prokina (soprano)
Anthony Rolfe Johnson (tenor)
Thomas Quastoff (baritone)
Royal Scottish National
   Orchestra Junior Chorus
Edinburgh Festival Chorus
Royal Scottish National Orchestra/
   Donald Runnicles

21 AUGUST 1996
Schoenberg: Gurrelieder
Jane Eaglen (Tove)
Marjana Lipovsek (Wood Dove)
Thomas Moser (Waldemar)
Kurt Azesberger (Klaus the Fool)
Franz Grundheber (Peasant)
Hans Hotter (narrator)
Arnold Schoenberg Choir
Edinburgh Festival Chorus
Gustav Mahler Jugendorchester/
  Claudio Abbado

25 AUGUST 1996
Haydn: The Creation
Felicity Lott (soprano)
John Mark Ainsley (tenor)
Neal Davies (baritone)
Edinburgh Festival Chorus
The Hanover Band/
  Sir Charles Mackerras

31 AUGUST 1996
Mendelssohn: Elijah
Bryn Terfel (Elijah)
Renée Fleming (Widow)
Libby Crabtree (second soprano)
Patricia Bardon (Angel)
Sara Fulgoni (Queen)
John Mark Ainsley (Obadiah)
John Bowen (Ahab)
Neal Davies (first bass)
Geoffrey Moses (second bass)
Matthew Munro (Youth)
Edinburgh Festival Chorus
Orchestra of the Age of
  Enlightenment/Paul Daniel
*Commercial recording made
in Caird Hall, Dundee*

1997

11 AUGUST 1997
Tippett: A Child of Our Time
Christine Brewer (soprano)
Michelle DeYoung (mezzo soprano)
Ian Bostridge (tenor)
Alastair Miles (bass)
Edinburgh Festival Chorus
Royal Scottish National Orchestra/
  Richard Armstrong

21 AUGUST 1997
Rossini: Petite messe solennelle
Nuccia Focile (soprano)
Michelle DeYoung (mezzo soprano)
Bruce Ford (tenor)
Alastair Miles (bass)
Edinburgh Festival Chorus
Royal Scottish National Orchestra/
  Carlo Rizzi

24 AUGUST 1997
Beethoven: Missa solemnis
Jane Eaglen (soprano)
Jane Irwin (mezzo soprano)
Thomas Moser (tenor)
Alastair Miles (bass)
Edinburgh Festival Chorus
Philharmonia Orchestra/
  Michael Gielen

30 AUGUST 1997
**Mahler: Symphony No 2
(Resurrection)**
Michèle Crider (soprano)
Markella Hatziano (mezzo soprano)
Edinburgh Festival Chorus
Oslo Philharmonic Orchestra/
  Mariss Jansons

1998

16 AUGUST 1998
Berlioz: Grande messe des morts
Gregory Turay (tenor)
Edinburgh Festival Chorus
Royal Scottish National Orchestra/
  Donald Runnicles

22 AUGUST 1998
Edinburgh Festival Theatre
Verdi: Giovanna d'Arco
Zvetelina Vassileva (Giovanna d'Arco)
Ian Storey (Delil)
Jean-Francis Monvoisin (Carlo VII)
Anthony Michaels-Moore (Giacomo)
Andrew Slater (Talbot)
Edinburgh Festival Chorus
Orchestra of Scottish Opera/
  Richard Armstrong

25 AUGUST 1998
**Beethoven: Symphony No 9
(Choral)**
Soile Isokoski (soprano)
Birgit Remmert (mezzo soprano)
Reiner Goldberg (tenor)
Eike Wilm Schulte (baritone)
Edinburgh Festival Chorus
Berlin Philharmonic Orchestra/
  Claudio Abbado

31 AUGUST 1998
Brahms: Ein deutsches Requiem
Karita Mattila (soprano)
Bryn Terfel (baritone)
Edinburgh Festival Chorus
Finnish Radio Symphony Orchestra/
  Jukka-Pekka Saraste

3 SEPTEMBER 1998
Beethoven: Choral Fantasia
Steven Osborne (piano)
Edinburgh Festival Chorus
Scottish Chamber Orchestra/
  Joseph Swensen

4 SEPTEMBER 1998
Edinburgh Festival Theatre
Smetana: Libuše
Eva Urbanová (Libuše)
Ivan Kusnjer (Přemysl)
Jiří Sulzenko (Chrudoš)
Štefan Margita (Šťáhlav)
Peter Mikuláš (Lutobor)
Jiří Kubík (Radovan)
Helena Kaupová (Krasava)
Denisa Šlepkovská (Radmila)
Edinburgh Festival Chorus
BBC Scottish Symphony Orchestra/
  Oliver von Dohnányi

1999

15 AUGUST 1999
Handel: Saul
Bryn Terfel (Saul)
Lisa Milne (Michal)
Joan Rodgers (Merab)
David Daniels (David)
Ian Bostridge (Jonathan)
Toby Spence (High Priest)
Neil Jenkins (Witch of Endor)
Neal Davies (Ghost of Samuel)
Thomas Trotter (organ)
Edinburgh Festival Chorus
Scottish Chamber Orchestra/
  Sir Charles Mackerras

21 AUGUST 1999
Verdi: Requiem
Amanda Roocroft (soprano)
Jane Irwin (mezzo soprano)
Ramón Vargas (tenor)
Eric Halfvarson (bass)
Edinburgh Festival Chorus
Swedish Radio Symphony Orchestra/
  Myung-Whun Chung

25 AUGUST 1999
Mahler: Symphony No 3
Michelle DeYoung (mezzo soprano)
Royal Scottish National
  Orchestra Junior Chorus
Edinburgh Festival Chorus (ladies)
BBC Symphony Orchestra/
  Bernard Haitink

27 AUGUST 1999
Rossini: Stabat Mater
Andrea Rost (soprano)
Lorraine Hunt Lieberson (soprano)
Stuart Neill (tenor)
Ildebrando d'Arcangelo (bass)
Edinburgh Festival Chorus
Royal Scottish National Orchestra/
  David Robertson

3 SEPTEMBER 1999
**Mahler: Symphony No 2
(Resurrection)**
Juliane Banse (soprano)
Birgit Remmert (mezzo soprano)
Edinburgh Festival Chorus
Vienna Philharmonic Orchestra/
  Sir Simon Rattle

2000

13 AUGUST 2000
Berlioz: The Damnation of Faust
Jennifer Larmore (Marguerite)
Bryn Terfel (Méphistophélès)
Neal Davies (Brander)
Vincent Cole (Faust)
Royal Scottish National
  Orchestra Junior Chorus
Cleveland Orchestra Chorus
Edinburgh Festival Chorus
Cleveland Orchestra/
  Christoph von Dohnányi

17 AUGUST 2000
Britten: Spring Symphony
Lisa Milne (soprano)
Catherine Wyn-Rogers
  (mezzo soprano)
Ian Bostridge (tenor)
Royal Scottish National
  Orchestra Junior Chorus
Edinburgh Festival Chorus
Royal Scottish National Orchestra/
  James MacMillan

23 AUGUST 2000
Mozart: Requiem
Janice Watson (soprano)
Imelda Drumm (mezzo soprano)
Jonas Kaufmann (tenor)
Phillip Ens (bass)
Edinburgh Festival Chorus
Budapest Festival Orchestra/
  Iván Fischer

29 AUGUST 2000
**Verdi: Four Sacred Pieces
Mahler: Das klagende Lied**
Hillevi Martinpelto (soprano)
Katerina Karnéus (mezzo soprano)
Nathan Gunn (baritone)
Jonas Kaufmann (tenor)
Libby Crabtree (soprano) (Knabe)
Oliver Carden (contralto) (Knabe)
Kathy Crawford (EFC) (contralto)
Tori Graham (EFC) (contralto)
Edinburgh Festival Chorus
Royal Scottish National Orchestra/
  Carlo Rizzi

2001

12 AUGUST 2001
**Berlioz: The Trojans Part 1,
  The Siege of Troy**
Petra Lang (Cassandre)
Michelle Walton (Ascagne)
Anna Burford (Hécube)
Hugh Smith (Énée)
Christopher Maltman (Chorèbe)
Paul Whelan (Panthée)
John Relyea (Ghost of Hector)
Gerard O'Connor (Priam)
Darren Abrahams (Hélenus)
Tim Mirfin (Soldat/Chef Grec)
Edinburgh Festival Chorus
BBC Scottish Symphony Orchestra
David Jones (assistant conductor)
Donald Runnicles (conductor)

13 AUGUST 2001
Mozart: Idomeneo
Ian Bostridge (Idomeneo)
Lisa Milne (Ilia)
Barbara Frittoli (Elettra)
Lorraine Hunt-Lieberson (Idamante)
Anthony Rolfe Johnson (Arbace)
Paul Charles Clarke (High Priest
  of Neptune)
John Relyea (Oracle)
Edinburgh Festival Chorus
Dunedin Consort
Scottish Chamber Orchestra/
  Sir Charles Mackerras
Commercial recording

Concert listings

18 AUGUST 2001
Berlioz: The Trojans Part 2,
The Trojans at Carthage
Lorraine Hunt-Lieberson (Didon)
Catherine Wyn-Rogers (Anna)
Michelle Walton (Ascagne)
Hugh Smith (Énée)
John Mark Ainsley (Hylas)
Paul Agnew (Iopas)
John Relyea (Narbal)
Paul Whelan (Panthé)
Tim Mirfin (Mercure/Trojan
   Captain/Sentinel I)
Jonathan Lemalu (Trojan
   Captain/Sentinel II)
Gerard O'Connor (Ghost of Priam)
Petra Lang (Ghost of Cassandre)
Christopher Maltman (Ghost of Chorèbe)
John Relyea (Ghost of Hector)
Edinburgh Festival Chorus
BBC Scottish Symphony Orchestra/
   Donald Runnicles

25 AUGUST 2001
Beethoven: Symphony No 6
(Pastoral); Piano Concerto No 4;
Symphony No 5; Ah! Perfido;
Sanctus and Gloria from
Mass in C; Choral Fantasia
Janice Watson (soprano)
Jane Irwin (mezzo soprano)
Toby Spence (tenor)
Neal Davies (bass)
François-Frédéric Guy (piano)
Edinburgh Festival Chorus
Royal Scottish National Orchestra/
   Günther Herbig
TV recording for BBC Knowledge channel

1 SEPTEMBER 2001
Messiaen: Saint François d'Assise
David Wilson-Johnson
   (Saint François)
Heidi Grant Murphy (L'Ange)
Toby Spence (Frère Massée)
Christopher Maltman (Frère Léon)
Stuart Kale (Le lépreux)
James Gilchrist (Frère Élie)
Frédéric Caton (Frère Bernard)
Ivor Klayman (EFC) (Frère Sylvestre)
Peter Cannell (EFC) (Frère Rufin)
Edinburgh Festival Chorus
Radio Filharmonisch Orkest Holland/
   Reinbert de Leeuw

2002

11 AUGUST 2002
Berlioz: Te Deum
Donald Kaasch (tenor)
Prague Philharmonic Choir
RSNO Junior Chorus
Edinburgh Festival Chorus
Royal Scottish National Orchestra/
   Christoph von Dohnányi

12 AUGUST 2002
Liszt: Faust Symphony
Jonas Kaufmann (tenor)
Viktoria Postnikova (piano)
Edinburgh Festival Chorus
   (gentlemen)
Royal Scottish National Orchestra/
   Gennady Rozhdestvensky

18 AUGUST 2002
Enescu: Oedipe
John Relyea (Oedipe)
Janice Watson (Antigone)
Catherine Wyn-Rogers
   (Jocaste/The Sphinx)
Anna Burford (Mérope)
Marius Brenciu (The Shepherd)
Norman Shankle (Laïos/Thésée)
Jonathan Lemalu (Créon)
Neal Davies (Tirésias)
Ionel Pantea (The Watchman)
Tim Mirfin (High Priest/Phorbas)
Kenneth Ballantine, Peter Cannell,
Elizabeth Currie, Dorothy Fairweather,
David Hewitson, Rea Johnston, Ivor
Klayman, Nancy Muir, Lesley Walker,
Richard Weddle & James White (EFC)
Edinburgh Festival Chorus
BBC Scottish Symphony Orchestra/
   Cristian Mandeal

21 AUGUST 2002
Adams: Harmonium
Edinburgh Festival Chorus
BBC Scottish Symphony Orchestra/
   David Jones

25 AUGUST 2002
Handel: Jephtha
Ian Bostridge (Jephtha)
Sarah Fox (Iphis)
Jane Irwin (Storgè)
Bejun Mehta (Hamor)
Jonathan Lemalu (Zebul)
Thomas Henderson (Angel)
Edinburgh Festival Chorus
Scottish Chamber Orchestra/
   Sir Charles Mackerras

31 AUGUST 2002
Dvořák: Saint Ludmila
Eva Urbanová (Saint Ludmila)
Dagmar Pecková (Svatava)
Peter Straka (Bořivoj)
Aleš Briscein (Rolník)
Peter Mikuláš (Saint Ivan)
Edinburgh Festival Chorus
Royal Scottish National Orchestra/
   Jiří Bělohlávek

2003

9 & 10 AUGUST 2003
Janáček: Glagolitic Mass
Christine Brewer (soprano)
Jane Irwin (mezzo soprano)
Glenn Winslade (tenor)
Neal Davies (bass)
Thomas Trotter (organ)
Edinburgh Festival Chorus
Royal Scottish National Orchestra/
   Sir Charles Mackerras

14 AUGUST 2003
Debussy: Nocturnes
Ravel: Daphnis et Chloé
Edinburgh Festival Chorus
Los Angeles Philharmonic Orchestra/
   Esa-Pekka Salonen

15 AUGUST 2003
Wagner: Lohengrin
Torsten Kerl (Lohengrin)
Hillevi Martinpelto (Elsa of Brabant)
Jukka Rasilainen (Friedrich
   von Telramund)
Petra Lang (Ortrud)
Eric Halfvarson (King Henry)
James Rutherford (Herald)
Campbell Russell, Declan
McCusker, Paul Anwyl, David
   Morrison plus members of EFC
   basses as Brabantine nobles
Philharmonia Chorus (tenors and basses)
Edinburgh Festival Chorus
BBC Scottish Symphony Orchestra/
   Donald Runnicles

22 AUGUST 2003
Mahler: Symphony No 2
(Resurrection)
Soile Isokoski (soprano)
Jane Irwin (mezzo soprano)
Edinburgh Festival Chorus
Royal Scottish National Orchestra/
   Garry Walker

27 AUGUST 2003
Verdi: Macbeth
Violeta Urmana (Lady Macbeth)
Mark Delavan (Macbeth)
Marius Brenciu (Macduff)
Alfredo Nigro (Malcolm)
John Relyea (Banquo)
Carole Wilson (Lady-in-waiting)
Tim Mirfin (Servant/Doctor)
Paul Anwyl (Murderer/Herald/Apparition)
Oliver Boyd (Apparition)
Thomas Henderson (Apparition)
Edinburgh Festival Chorus
Scottish Chamber Orchestra/
   Sir Charles Mackerras

2004

15 AUGUST 2004
Honegger: Jeanne d'Arc au bûcher
Jeanne Balibar (Jeanne d'Arc)
Philippe Girard (Brother Dominique)
Lisa Milne (Marguerite)
Sarah Fox (The Virgin)
Jane Irwin (Catherine)
Paul Agnew (Porcus/First Herald/Cleric)
Tim Mirfin (Second Herald/Peasant)
Michel Fau (Third Herald)
John Arnold (Duke of Bedford)
Jean-François Perrier
   (John of Luxembourg)
Damien Bigourdan (Usher)
Nazim Boudjenah (Regnault de Chartres)
Christophe Maltot (Guillaume de Flavy)
Guillaume Durieux (Perrot)
Miloud Khétib (Priest)
Pierre-André Weitz (Ass)
Elizabeth Mazev (Mother of Barrels)
Olivier Balazuc (Heurtebise)
Bruno Sermonne (Peasant)
Centre Dramatique National/Orléans-
   Loiret-Centre (Olivier Py, director)
Valérie Hartmann-Claverie
   (ondes martenot)
Royal Scottish National Orchestra
   Junior Chorus
Edinburgh Festival Chorus
Royal Scottish National Orchestra/
   Kwamé Ryan

19 AUGUST 2004
Weber: Euryanthe
Gabriele Fontana (Euryanthe)
Christine Brewer (Eglantine)
Stewart Skelton (Adolar)
Neal Davies (Lysiart)
Alfred Reiter (King Ludwig)
Gail Johnston (Bertha)
Campbell Russell (Rudolph)
Edinburgh Festival Chorus
BBC Scottish Symphony Orchestra/
   David Robertson

29 AUGUST 2004
MacMillan: Quickening
(Scottish premiere)
Hilliard Ensemble
John Kitchen (grand organ)
John Langdon (chamber organ)
Royal Scottish National Orchestra
   Junior Chorus
Edinburgh Festival Chorus
Royal Scottish National Orchestra/
   Garry Walker

3 SEPTEMBER 2004
Britten: War Requiem
Olga Guryakova (soprano)
Mark Padmore (tenor)
Christian Gerhaher (bass)
NYCoS National Boys Choir
Edinburgh Festival Chorus
Paragon Ensemble/Garry Walker
BBC Scottish Symphony Orchestra/
   Ilan Volkov

2005

14 AUGUST 2005
Verdi: Requiem
Violeta Urmana (soprano)
Leandra Overmann (mezzo soprano)
Salvatore Licitra (tenor)
John Relyea (bass)
Edinburgh Festival Chorus
BBC Scottish Symphony Orchestra/
   Donald Runnicles

18 August 2005
Mahler: Symphony No 3
Birgitta Svenden (mezzo soprano)
Royal Scottish National
   Orchestra Junior Chorus
Edinburgh Festival Chorus (ladies)
BBC Scottish Symphony Orchestra/
   Donald Runnicles

21 August 2005
Prokofiev: War and Peace Suite
Tchaikovsky: 1812 Overture
Edinburgh Festival Chorus
Tchaikovsky Symphony Orchestra of
   Moscow Radio/Vladimir Fedoseyev

27 August 2005
Beethoven: Mass in C
Beethoven: Christ on the Mount of Olives
Rebecca Bottone (soprano)
Karen Cargill (mezzo soprano)
Pavol Breslik (tenor)
Alfred Reiter (bass)
Edinburgh Festival Chorus
Royal Scottish National Orchestra/
David Robertson

30 August 2005
Wagner: Tristan und Isolde
Christine Brewer (Isolde)
Jane Irwin (Brangäne)
Christian Franz (Tristan)
Juha Uusitalo (Kurwenal)
John Relyea (King Mark)
Edinburgh Festival
Chorus (gentlemen)
Bamberg Symphony Orchestra/
Jonathan Nott

2006

13 August 2006
Strauss: Elektra
Jeanne-Michele Charbonnet (Elektra)
Leandra Overmann (Klytemnaestra)
Silvana Dussmann (Chrysothemis)
Matthew Rose (Tutor)
Iain Paterson (Orestes)
Ian Storey (Aegisthus)
Miriam Murphy (Overseer)
Anna Burford (First Maid)
Liane Keegan (Second Maid)
Karen Cargill (Third Maid)
Rachel Hynes (Fourth Maid)
Sarah-Jane Davies (Fifth Maid)
Elizabeth Currie (Confidante)
Alison Beck (Trainbearer)
Robert Murray (Young Servant)
Peter Cannell (Old Servant)
Edinburgh Festival Chorus
Royal Scottish National Orchestra/
Edward Gardner

17 August 2006
Vaughan Williams: Serenade to Music; Dona nobis pacem
Claire Booth (soprano)
Ha Young Lee (soprano)
Lee Bisset (soprano)
Kate Valentine (soprano)
Louise Mott (mezzo soprano)
Anna Stéphany (mezzo soprano)
Madeline Shaw (mezzo soprano)
Doreen Curran (mezzo soprano)
Robert Murray (tenor)
Benjamin Segal (tenor)
Adrian Dwyer (tenor)
Ed Lyon (tenor)
Garry Magee (baritone)
Roland Wood (baritone)
Tim Mirfin (bass)
David Soar (bass)
Edinburgh Festival Chorus
Scottish Chamber Orchestra/
David Jones

18 AUGUST 2006
Rossini: La donna del lago
Carmen Giannattasio (Elena)
Kenneth Tarver (Giacomo)
Patricia Bardon (Malcolm Groeme)
Gregory Kunde (Rodrigo)
Robert Gleadow (Douglas d'Angus)
Francesca Sassu (Albina)
Mark Wilde (Serano/Betram)
Edinburgh Festival Chorus
Scottish Chamber Orchestra/
Maurizio Benini

21 AUGUST 2006
Schumann: Manfred
Mark Waschke (Manfred)
Lucy Crowe (Astarte)
Anna Stéphany (Witch of the Alps)
Robert Murray (Spirit)
Neal Davies (Chamois Hunter/Abbot)
Matthew Rose (Nemesis)
Robert Winslade Anderson (Ariman)
Robert Gleadow (bass)
Edinburgh Festival Chorus
BBC Scottish Symphony Orchestra/
Ilan Volkov

1 SEPTEMBER 2006
Beethoven: Symphony No 9 (Choral)
Janice Watson (soprano)
Catherine Wyn-Rogers
(mezzo soprano)
Stuart Skelton (tenor)
Detlef Roth (baritone)
Edinburgh Festival Chorus
Philharmonia Orchestra/
Sir Charles Mackerras
BBC Radio 3 broadcast

2 SEPTEMBER 2006
Wagner: Die Meistersinger von Nürnberg
Hillevi Martinpelto (Eva)
Jonas Kaufmann (Walther
von Stolzing)
Toby Spence (David)
Wendy Dawn Thompson (Magdalene)
Paul Whelan (Nightwatchman)
Robert Holl (Hans Sachs)
Andrew Shore (Sextus Beckmesser)
Matthew Rose (Veit Pogner)
James Rutherford (Fritz Kothner)
William Kendall (Kunz Vogelgesang)
John Shirley-Quirk (Konrad Nachtigal)
Jeffrey Lawton (Balthasar Zorn)
John Mitchinson (Ulrich Eisslinger)
John Robertson (Augustin Moser)
Phillip Joll (Hermann Ortel)
Glenville Hargreaves (Hans Schwartz)
Richard Van Allan (Hans Foltz)
Members of the Alexander Gibson
Opera School, RSAMD, also took
part in the performance
Edinburgh Festival Chorus
BBC Scottish Symphony Orchestra/
David Robertson

2007

Festival Director:
Jonathan Mills (2007–2014)

10 AUGUST 2007
Bernstein: Candide
Matthew Polenzani (Candide)
Laura Aikin (Cunegonde)
Thomas Allen (Doctor Pangloss/
Martin/Narrator)
Keith Lewis (Governor/
Vanderdendur/Ragotski)
Kathryn Harries (Old Lady)
Jennifer Johnston (Paquette)
Tim Mirfin (Bearkeeper/
Inquisitor/Tsar Ivan)
Roland Wood (Maximilian/Captain)
James Geer (Cosmetic Merchant/
Prince Charles Edward)
Ronald Nairne (Doctor/
Inquisitor/King Stanislaus)
Richard Latham (Junkman/
Inquisitor/King Hermann Augustus)
Andrew Dickinson (Alchemist/
Inquisitor/Sultan Achmet/Crook)
Edinburgh Festival Chorus
BBC Scottish Symphony Orchestra/
Robert Spano

20 AUGUST 2007
Haydn: The Creation
Katharine Fuge (soprano)
Anne Lewis (contralto)
Ian Bostridge (tenor)
Matthew Rose (bass)
Edinburgh Festival Chorus
Scottish Chamber Orchestra/
Sir Roger Norrington

23 August 2007
Stravinsky: Oedipus rex
Jeffrey Lloyd-Roberts (Oedipus)
Natascha Petrinksy (Jocasta)
Terje Stensvold (Creon)
Matthew Rose (Tiresias)
Andrew Kennedy (Shepherd)
Neal Davies (Messenger)
Simon Russell Beale (Narrator)
Edinburgh Festival Chorus (gentlemen)
BBC Scottish Symphony Orchestra/
Susanna Mälkki

1 SEPTEMBER 2007
Poulenc: Stabat Mater
Christine Brewer (soprano)
Poulenc: Dialogues des Carmélites (excerpts)
Rosemary Joshua (Blanche de la Force)
Rebecca Bottone (Soeur Constance)
Thomas Walker (Le Chevalier de la Force)
Tove Dahlberg (Mère Marie)
Liane Keegan (La Prieure)
James Geer (L'Aumônier)
Hélène Racineux (Soeur Mathilde)
Louise Collett (Mère Jeanne)
Bronagh Byrne, Natalie Montakhab,
Catharine Rodgers, Kirstin Sharpin,
Clare Tucker, Emilie Alford, Maria
Brown, Laura Kelly, Elysia Leech,
Una McMahon, Emily Mitchell
Edinburgh Festival Chorus
Royal Scottish National Orchestra/
Stéphane Denève

2008

Chorus Master:
Christopher Bell (2008 to date)

3 JUNE 2008
Edinburgh, Palace of Holyrood, Throne Room In the presence of HRH Prince Charles and the Duchess of Cornwall
Tippett: Spirituals from A Child of Our Time
28 members of the Edinburgh
Festival Chorus/Michael Bawtree

8 AUGUST 2008
Weill: The Rise and Fall of the City of Mahagonny
Susan Bickley (Leokadja Begbick)
Jeffrey Lloyd-Roberts (Fatty)
Alan Opie (Trinity Moses)
Giselle Allen (Jenny Hill)
Anthony Dean Griffey
(Jimmy Mahoney)
Peter Hoare (Jack Smith/
Toby Higgins)
Stephan Loges (Bill)
Brindley Sherratt (Joe)
Ladies of RSAMD (Girls
of Mahagonny)
Edinburgh Festival
Chorus (gentlemen)
Royal Scottish National Orchestra/
HK Gruber

13 AUGUST 2008
Handel: Israel in Egypt
Lucy Crowe (soprano)
Claire Debono (soprano)
Robin Blaze (countertenor)
Mark Tucker (tenor)
Matthew Brook (bass)
Henry Waddington (bass)
Edinburgh Festival Chorus
Scottish Chamber Orchestra/
Emmanuelle Haïm

18 AUGUST 2008
Honegger: Le roi David
Geraldine McGreevy (soprano)
Karen Cargill (mezzo soprano)
Yann Beuron (tenor)
Sylvia Bergé (La Pythonisse)
Seamus Herron (David as a child)
Andrej Seweryn (Narrator)
Edinburgh Festival Chorus
Royal Scottish National Orchestra/
Stéphane Denève

30 AUGUST 2008
Tippett: A Child of Our Time
Nicole Cabell (soprano)
Jane Irwin (mezzo soprano)
John Mark Ainsley (tenor)
Sir John Tomlinson (bass)
Edinburgh Festival Chorus
BBC Scottish Symphony Orchestra/
Gennady Rozhdestvensky

Concert listings

2009

14 AUGUST 2009
Handel: Judas Maccabaeus
William Burden (Judas Maccabaeus)
Rosemary Joshua (Israelitish Woman)
Sarah Connolly (Israelitish Man)
Neal Davies (Simon/
 Eupolemus/Messenger)
Reno Troilus (Messenger)
Edinburgh Festival Chorus
Scottish Chamber Orchestra/
 William Christie

21 August 2009
Verdi: Macbeth
Susan Neves (Lady Macbeth)
Lado Ataneli (Macbeth)
Vsevolod Grivnov (Macduff)
Nicholas Phan (Malcolm)
John Relyea (Banquo)
Katherine Broderick (Lady-in-waiting)
Vuyani Mlinde (Servant/Doctor)
Wade Kernot (Herald/
 Murderer/Apparition)
Michael Yeoman (NYCoS National
 Boys Choir) (Apparition)
Niall Docherty (NYCoS National
 Boys Choir) (Apparition)
Edinburgh Festival Chorus
BBC Scottish Symphony Orchestra/
 David Robertson

28 AUGUST 2009
Berlioz: Roméo et Juliette
Patricia Bardon (mezzo soprano)
Loïc Félix (tenor)
Franz Hawlata (bass)
Edinburgh Festival Chorus
Royal Scottish National Orchestra/
 Stéphane Denève

5 SEPTEMBER 2009
Elgar: The Dream of Gerontius
Alice Coote (mezzo soprano)
Paul Groves (tenor)
Iain Paterson (bass)
John Kitchen (organ)
National Youth Choir of Scotland
Edinburgh Festival Chorus
Hallé Orchestra/Sir Mark Elder

15 OCTOBER 2009
Glasgow, City Halls
Ravel: Daphnis et Chloé
Edinburgh Festival Chorus
BBC Scottish Symphony Orchestra/
 Donald Runnicles
Broadcast on BBC Radio 3

16 OCTOBER 2009
Perth, Concert Hall
Ravel: Daphnis et Chloé
Edinburgh Festival Chorus
BBC Scottish Symphony Orchestra/
 Donald Runnicles

2010

4 AUGUST 2010
London, Royal Albert Hall
Mahler: Symphony No 3
Karen Cargill (mezzo soprano)
Royal Scottish National Orchestra
 Junior Chorus
Edinburgh Festival Chorus (ladies)
BBC Scottish Symphony Orchestra/
 Donald Runnicles
Broadcast live on BBC Radio 3

13 AUGUST 2010
Adams: El niño
Jessica Rivera (soprano)
Kelley O'Connor (mezzo soprano)
Willard White (bass-baritone)
Robin Blaze (countertenor)
Paul Flight (countertenor)
William Purefoy (countertenor)
NYCoS National Girls Choir
Edinburgh Festival Chorus
BBC Scottish Symphony Orchestra/
 James Conlon

23 AUGUST 2010
Puccini: La fanciulla del West
Susan Bullock (Minnie)
Carl Tanner (Dick Johnson/Ramerrez)
Juha Uusitalo (Jack Rance)
Colin Judson (Nick)
Brindley Sherratt (Ashby)
Roland Wood (Sonora)
David Morrison (Billy Jackrabbit)
Louise Collett (Wowkle)
Steven Faughey (Jake Wallace)
Bruce Davis (Trin)
Phil Gault (Sid)
Paul Anwyl (Bello)
Paul Featherstone (Harry)
Nick Hardy (Joe)
Jonathan Sedgwick (Happy)
Anders Östberg (Larkens)
David Morrison (José Castro)
Declan McCusker (Pony Express rider)
Edinburgh Festival Chorus
 (gentlemen)
Orchestra of Scottish Opera/
 Francesco Corti

31 AUGUST 2010
Mahler: Symphony No 3
Anna Larsson (mezzo soprano)
Royal Scottish National
 Orchestra Junior Chorus
Edinburgh Festival Chorus (ladies)
Royal Concertgebouw Orchestra/
 Mariss Jansons

4 SEPTEMBER 2010
Mahler: Symphony No 8
Erin Wall (soprano)
Hillevi Martinpelto (soprano)
Nicole Cabell (soprano)
Katarina Karnéus (mezzo soprano)
Catherine Wyn-Rogers
 (mezzo soprano)
Simon O'Neill (tenor)
Anthony Michaels-Moore (baritone)
John Relyea (bass)
Royal Scottish National Orchestra
 Junior Chorus
Edinburgh Festival Chorus
BBC Scottish Symphony Orchestra/
 Donald Runnicles

10 OCTOBER 2010
**Usher Hall Gala Concert
 Official re-opening of the Usher
 Hall after refurbishment
Holst: The Planets**
Edinburgh Festival Chorus (ladies)
Houston Symphony Orchestra/
 Hans Graf

2011

10 FEBRUARY 2011
Glasgow, City Halls
Brahms: Ein deutsches Requiem
Lisa Milne (soprano)
Markus Brück (baritone)
Edinburgh Festival Chorus
BBC Scottish Symphony Orchestra/
 Donald Runnicles
Broadcast live on BBC Radio 3

13 FEBRUARY 2011
Edinburgh, Usher Hall
Brahms: Ein deutsches Requiem
Lisa Milne (soprano)
Markus Brück (baritone)
Edinburgh Festival Chorus
BBC Scottish Symphony Orchestra/
 Donald Runnicles

3 AUGUST 2011
London, Royal Albert Hall
Ravel: Daphnis et Chloé
Edinburgh Festival Chorus
BBC Scottish Symphony Orchestra/
 Donald Runnicles
Broadcast live on BBC Radio 3

12 AUGUST 2011
**Schumann: Das Paradies
 und die Peri**
Susan Gritton (Peri)
Maximilian Schmitt (Narrator)
Lydia Teuscher (Maiden)
Marie-Claude Chappuis (Angel)
Benjamin Hulett (Young Man)
Florian Boesch (Gazna/Man)
Edinburgh Festival Chorus
Scottish Chamber Orchestra/
 Sir Roger Norrington

18 AUGUST 2011
Massenet: Thaïs
Erin Wall (Thaïs)
Quinn Kelsey (Athanaël)
Eric Cutler (Nicias)
Stefano Palatchi (Palemon)
Stacey Tappan (La Charmeuse)
Sarah-Jane Brandon (Crobyle)
Clara Mouriz (Myrtale)
Clare Shearer (Albine)
Donald Thomson (Servant)
Kenneth Allen, Peter Cannell,
 David Hewitson & Ivor
 Klayman (EFC) (baritones)
Edinburgh Festival Chorus
Royal Scottish National Orchestra/
 Sir Andrew Davis

26 AUGUST 2011
Liszt: Faust Symphony
Kim Begley (tenor)
Edinburgh Festival Chorus
 (gentlemen)
Orchestra of the Age of
 Enlightenment/Vladimir Jurowski

28 AUGUST 2011
**Mahler: Symphony No 2
 (Resurrection)**
Meagan Miller (soprano)
Karen Cargill (mezzo soprano)
Edinburgh Festival Chorus
BBC Scottish Symphony Orchestra/
 Donald Runnicles

2 SEPTEMBER 2011
**Bartók: The Miraculous
 Mandarin**
Edinburgh Festival Chorus
Bamberg Symphony Orchestra/
 Jonathan Nott

3 SEPTEMBER 2011
Ravel: Daphnis et Chloé
Edinburgh Festival Chorus
Bamberg Symphony Orchestra/
 Jonathan Nott

2012

22 MARCH 2012
Glasgow, City Halls
Brahms: Alto Rhapsody
Sarah Connolly (mezzo soprano)
Edinburgh Festival Chorus
 (gentlemen)
BBC Scottish Symphony Orchestra/
 Donald Runnicles

25 MARCH 2012
Edinburgh, Usher Hall
Brahms: Alto Rhapsody
Sarah Connolly (mezzo soprano)
Edinburgh Festival Chorus
 (gentlemen)
BBC Scottish Symphony Orchestra/
 Donald Runnicles
Live broadcast on BBC Radio 3

10 AUGUST 2012
Delius: A Mass of Life
Anna Christy (soprano)
Pamela Helen Stephen
(mezzo soprano)
Robert Murray (tenor)
Hanno Müller-Brachmann (bass)
Edinburgh Festival Chorus
Royal Scottish National Orchestra/
Sir Andrew Davis

14 AUGUST 2012
*Due to a power failure at the Usher
Hall, the concert was cancelled at
8.15pm, the first time this has ever
happened to an EFC performance.*
Rachmaninov: The Bells
Tatiana Monogarova (soprano)
Sergey Skorokhodov (tenor)
Alexander Vinogradov (baritone)
Edinburgh Festival Chorus
London Philharmonic Orchestra/
Vladimir Jurowski

18 AUGUST 2012
**Szymanowski: Symphony No 3
(Song of the Night)**
Steve Davislim (tenor)
Edinburgh Festival Chorus
London Symphony Orchestra/
Valery Gergiev

23 AUGUST 2012
**Debussy: Nocturnes
Busoni: Piano Concerto**
Garrick Ohlsson (piano)
Edinburgh Festival Chorus
European Union Youth Orchestra/
Gianandrea Noseda

1 SEPTEMBER 2012
Walton: Belshazzar's Feast
Neal Davies (baritone)
Edinburgh Festival Chorus
Royal Scottish National Orchestra/
David Robertson

2013

9 AUGUST 2013
Prokofiev: Alexander Nevsky
Yulia Matochkina (mezzo soprano)
Edinburgh Festival Chorus
Royal Scottish National Orchestra/
Valery Gergiev

12 AUGUST 2013
**Mahler: Symphony No 2
(Resurrection)**
Genia Kühmeier (soprano)
Gerhild Romberger (mezzo soprano)
Edinburgh Festival Chorus
Bavarian Radio Symphony Orchestra/
Mariss Jansons

20 AUGUST 2013
Scriabin: Symphony No 1
Svetlana Sozdateleva (soprano)
Maxim Paster (tenor)
Edinburgh Festival Chorus
Russian National Orchestra/
Mikhail Pletnev

26 AUGUST 2013
Brahms: Ein deutsches Requiem
Rachel Harnisch (soprano)
Florian Boesch (baritone)
Edinburgh Festival Chorus
Tonhalle Orchestra Zurich/
David Zinman

31 AUGUST 2013
Verdi: Requiem
Erin Wall (soprano)
Karen Cargill (mezzo soprano)
Brian Hymel (tenor)
Eric Owens (bass-baritone)
Edinburgh Festival Chorus
BBC Scottish Symphony Orchestra/
Donald Runnicles

2014

15 MAY 2014
Glasgow, City Halls
**Vaughan Williams:
A Sea Symphony**
Elizabeth Watts (soprano)
Mark Stone (baritone)
Edinburgh Festival Chorus
BBC Scottish Symphony Orchestra/
Andrew Manze
Live broadcast on BBC Radio 3

8 AUGUST 2014
**Debussy: Le martyre
de Saint Sébastien
Scriabin: Prometheus –
The Poem of Fire**
Claire Booth (soprano)
Clare McCaldin (mezzo soprano)
Polly May (mezzo soprano)
Kirill Gerstein (piano)
Edinburgh Festival Chorus
Royal Scottish National Orchestra/
Oliver Knussen
BBC Radio 3 broadcast

9 AUGUST 2014
**Holst: The Planets
Colin Matthews: Pluto**
Edinburgh Festival Chorus (ladies)
BBC Scottish Symphony Orchestra/
Donald Runnicles

10 AUGUST 2014
**World War 1 Commemoration
Scotland Drumhead Service,
Edinburgh Castle Esplanade in
the presence of First Minister
Alex Salmond and the Lord
Provost of Edinburgh
Holst: Turn Back, O Man
Hymns**
National Youth Choir of Scotland
Stewart's Melville School Choir
Edinburgh Festival Chorus
Military bands from the Royal
Navy, Royal Air Force and Army
Live television broadcast

14 AUGUST 2014
Britten: War Requiem
Albina Shagimuratova (soprano)
Toby Spence (tenor)
Matthias Goerne (baritone)
NYCoS National Boys Choir
Edinburgh Festival Chorus
Philharmonia Orchestra/
Sir Andrew Davis

24 AUGUST 2014
Bernstein: Kaddish Symphony
Rebecca Evans (soprano)
Samuel Pisar (narrator)
NYCoS National Girls Choir
Edinburgh Festival Chorus
Royal Scottish National Orchestra/
John Axelrod

30 AUGUST 2014
**Mills: Sandakan Threnody
Janáček: Glagolitic Mass**
Hibla Gerzmava (soprano)
Claudia Huckle (contralto)
Simon O'Neill (tenor)
Andrew Staples (tenor)
Ivor Klayman (EFC) (baritone)
Jan Martinik (bass)
Thomas Trotter (organ)
BBC Scottish Symphony Orchestra/
Ilan Volkov

13 NOVEMBER 2014
Glasgow, City Halls
**Beethoven: Symphony No 9
(Choral)**
Angela Meade (soprano)
Elizabeth Bishop (mezzo soprano)
Stuart Skelton (tenor)
Marko Mimica (bass-baritone)
Edinburgh Festival Chorus
BBC Scottish Symphony Orchestra/
Donald Runnicles
*Live BBC Radio 3 broadcast
and television recording*

14 NOVEMBER 2014
Aberdeen, Music Hall
**Beethoven: Symphony No 9
(Choral)**
Angela Meade (soprano)
Elizabeth Bishop (mezzo soprano)
Stuart Skelton (tenor)
Marko Mimica (bass-baritone)
Edinburgh Festival Chorus
BBC Scottish Symphony Orchestra/
Donald Runnicles

16 NOVEMBER 2014
Edinburgh, Usher Hall
**Beethoven: Symphony No 9
(Choral)**
Angela Meade (soprano)
Elizabeth Bishop (mezzo soprano)
Stuart Skelton (tenor)
Marko Mimica (bass-baritone)
Edinburgh Festival Chorus
BBC Scottish Symphony Orchestra/
Donald Runnicles

2015

**Festival Director:
Fergus Linehan (2015 to date)**

**50th Anniversary of the
Edinburgh Festival Chorus**

7 AUGUST 2015
**Beethoven: Choral Fantasy
Adams: Harmonium**
Rudolf Buchbinder (piano)
Edinburgh Festival Chorus
Royal Scottish National Orchestra/
Peter Oundjian

8 AUGUST 2015
**Brahms: Gesang der Parzen;
Liebeslieder Waltzer;
Schickalslied**
Edinburgh Festival Chorus
BBC Scottish Symphony Orchestra/
Donald Runnicles

14 AUGUST 2015
Sibelius: Kullervo
Anna Larsson (mezzo soprano)
Johan Reuter (bass-baritone)
RSNO Chorus
Edinburgh Festival Chorus
(gentlemen)
Royal Scottish National Orchestra/
Edward Gardner

18 AUGUST 2015
Mozart: Requiem
Miah Persson (soprano)
Barbara Kozelj (mezzo soprano)
Jeremy Ovenden (tenor)
Konstantin Wolff (bass)
Edinburgh Festival Chorus
Budapest Festival Orchestra/
Iván Fischer

22 AUGUST 2015
Berlioz: Grande messe des morts
Lawrence Brownlee (tenor)
Edinburgh Festival Chorus
Philharmonia Orchestra/
Esa-Pekka Salonen

29 AUGUST 2015
Beethoven: Missa solemnis
Genia Kuhmeier (soprano)
Alice Coote (mezzo soprano)
Michael Schade (tenor)
Georg Zeppenfeld (bass)
Edinburgh Festival Chorus
Scottish Chamber Orchestra/
Robin Ticciati

The EFC's records, CDs and DVDs

1967

The Cambridge Hymnal
Arthur Oldham (conductor)
EMI/HMV mono CLP 3598

1969

Mozart: Complete Masonic Music
London Symphony Orchestra/
István Kertész
Decca SXL 6409

Kodály: Háry János
London Symphony Orchestra/
István Kertész
Decca ZAL 8706/9

1972

Brahms: Ein deutsches Requiem
London Philharmonic Orchestra/
Daniel Barenboim
*Deutsche Grammophon
Z2530–200/300*

1973

Mahler: Symphony No 2 (Resurrection)
London Symphony Orchestra/
Leonard Bernstein
CBS 78249

1974

Fauré: Requiem
Orchestre de Paris/
Daniel Barenboim
EMI/HMV A4ASD 34065

Fauré: Pavane
Orchestre de Paris/
Daniel Barenboim
EMI CDM 64634 2 (re-release)

1987

Berlioz: The Damnation of Faust
Orchestre de l'Opéra de Lyon/
John Eliot Gardiner
Phillips 426 199–2

1990

**Scottish Power
An Evening with the Edinburgh Festival Chorus and the Power of Scotland Pipe Band**
Selected Scottish folk songs together with choral music by Brahms and Verdi

1993

Mozart: Così fan tutte
Scottish Chamber Orchestra/
Sir Charles Mackerras
Telarc CD–80360

1995

Zimmermann: Requiem for a Young Poet
SWF Sinfonieorchester,
Baden-Baden/Michael Gielen
Sony Classical SK 61995
Also DVD documentary recording by WDR Cologne

1996

Beethoven: Fidelio
Scottish Chamber Orchestra/
Sir Charles Mackerras
Telarc CD–80439

Mendelssohn: Elijah
Orchestra of the Age of Enlightenment/Paul Daniel
Decca 455 688–2

2001

Mozart: Idomeneo
Scottish Chamber Orchestra/
Sir Charles Mackerras
EMI 7243 5 57260 5

Verdi: Requiem
London Symphony Orchestra/
Claudio Abbado
DVD recording:
Arthaus Musik 100146
Recorded 1982

2005

Janáček: The Eternal Gospel
BBC Scottish Symphony Orchestra/Ilan Volkov
Hyperion CDA 67517

2005

Mahler: Symphony No 2 (Resurrection)
London Symphony Orchestra/
Leonard Bernstein
*DVD box set of Bernstein Mahler symphonies including 1972 EFC performance at Ely Cathedral
Deutsche Grammophon 0734088*

2007

Rossini: La donna del lago
Scottish Chamber Orchestra/
Maurizio Benini
Opera Rara ORC–34
Recorded 2006

2011

Mahler: Symphony No 8
BBC Scottish Symphony Orchestra/Donald Runnicles
*BBC Music Magazine BBCMM330
vol 19 no 7, April 2011
Recorded 2010*

2013

Britten: War Requiem
BBC Scottish Symphony Orchestra/Donald Runnicles
*BBC Music Magazine BBCMM353
vol 21 no 4, January 2013
Recorded 2004*

Brahms: Ein deutsches Requiem
BBC Scottish Symphony Orchestra/Donald Runnicles
*BBC Music Magazine BBCMM358
vol 21 no 9, June 2013
Recorded 2011*

2014

Beethoven: Missa solemnis
London Philharmonic Orchestra/
Sir Georg Solti
LPO 0077
Recorded 1982